I'm not perfect
but that's ok

By Michelle Bailey

*Just another book full of encouraging blogs
and thoughts*

I'm Not Perfect But That's Ok

Authored by Michelle Bailey

Acknowledgement

I dedicate this book to all those who thought
and said I would amount to nothing. Thank you
for allowing me to prove you wrong.

About the author

Michelle Bailey from Birmingham UK has been writing since 1996 and has published 3 blog blogs and 4 poetry books. Michelle who holds a degree in Business Administration with Human Resource Management works as a Benefit Officer with a Local Authority.

As a woman of faith with a Certificate in Theology, the author writes honestly about her feelings and experiences with the aim of helping others find inner peace. Having been a practising Christian since 1998, she is a member of Muntz St New Testament Church of God.

Michelle aged 46 has a passion and gift for writing, she is the mother of a 24-year son, Michelle's own mother died when she was only nine months old and also lost her she sister when she was 17 years of age. A childhood, brought up in a care home from the age of 9 months to sis years of age and then Michelle was fostered until the age of fourteen to then return to a children's home until she eighteen. Michelle struggled to live independently and has suffered with her mental health for many years; her writing helps the reader to gain some understanding of the experience of who she is and living with a mental illness.

Content

Vinegar

I'll never forget when someone asked me to try balsamic vinegar. I categorically said no I don't like it. I had never tried it before, but I knew I wouldn't like it, needless to say when I eventually tried it I actually liked it. My son bless him when he was younger wouldn't eat the crusts of his bread, he declared that WE don't like them, bearing in mind he had never tried them, he saw that I didn't eat them, and decided he won't eat them too.

There's lots of things I haven't tried, I wanted to be a midwife, but fear started to show me all that could go wrong so I didn't even try to apply for the course. I've not tried risotto because it looks wet, and I don't like wet rice. I haven't tried bungee jumping as it looks dangerous. Sometimes it's easier not to try something in case you feel you may fail, it can prevent us from doing things that we need to, that we may enjoy or not enjoy. Trying can bring about failure and that's just a part of life, but on the other hand it can also bring success.

What I suppose I'm saying is that there may be many of us who haven't tried Jesus. Maybe we have heard things about Him, seen how the world is, watched loved one's die, lost a job, got divorced etc. But you know what.... there is so much that you are missing... in **Psalm 34:8 it says taste and see that the LORD is good; blessed is the one who takes refuge in him.** In that verse to me it is saying to taste, and in order to taste you need to try and once you have tasted you will see that it is good.

Try God today...try him for your miracle, for your breakthrough, for all that you need, not want but need.

The Pit

My son's room resembles what I call a pit, I'm unsure if he knows what a wardrobe is for due to the fact that all his clothes are on the floor or his chair, his 'I'll do it later' has no time limit, sometimes a month later I'm still waiting, he will walk around in boxer shorts but declare he is freezing and demand the central heating be put on, he has stated he is going to buy paper plates and plastic cups because he hates washing up and when I say have you any dirty clothes and the reply is no, I get a bit flabbergasted that after doing a half load of washing, lo and behold poof dirty clothes appear.

I suppose what I'm saying is that there's things my son does that winds me up and I don't understand why he does them, but I don't love him any less, I may get frustrated, we may argue, we may stop talking to each other for a while, but on the same hand there's things that I do that God must be thinking 'Michelle, why,' or my 'I'll do it later' never comes. God may be saying to me, bring all your dirty stuff to me so I can cleanse you and I'm like I haven't got none, but if I was to look deep inside there's probably a basket full. But in all of this, God doesn't love me any less, He doesn't fall out with me, doesn't stop talking to me, I may stop talking and listening to Him, but just like I want the best for my son and see the potential he has, God wants the best for me, his daughter, He sees the potential I have and just as I wait patiently for my son to do the things he has said he will do, God is patient with me/us

2 Peter 3:9 The Lord is not slow in keeping his promise, as some understand slowness. Instead, he is patient with you, not wanting anyone to perish, but everyone to come to repentance.

Psalm 90:4 A thousand years in your sight are like a day that has just gone by, or like a watch in the night.

Flare Up

For the last few days my IBS has flared up and I have been suffering with really terrible stomach cramps, kind of like when I was in labour and it got me thinking, when I was in labour and for the many thousand others who have as well, we swear blind we are not putting ourselves through that kind of pain, but, some women do because once the baby is born they forget about the pain, so even though we know we are going to suffer, but we look down at our new-born and we say you know what, my child is worth it and yes I would do it again.

There's a song that Tasha Cobbs sings, and it says those same words "you are beautiful my lovely creation, can't take my eyes off you, He said It was all worth it, and yes, I would do it again"

To me it this means that here is God saying, we are beautiful, we are His lovely creation and as much as it hurt Him to send Jesus to die and as much as Jesus suffered, they are saying, you/I/we/us was worth it and yes, I would send Jesus to die again.

Be blessed today

Quicksand

The thing with quicksand is its very deceiving, in approaching it may look like normal sand/mud but once you step into it..........

I have seen loads of movies where someone has stepped in quicksand and in a blink of an eye they're almost covered up to the neck in mud and on the verge of being pulled under, so they flail they're arms about in desperation to get out, but it only makes them sink further! However, according to the internet continued or panicked movement, however, may cause a person in quicksand to sink deeper, leading to belief that quicksand is dangerous. Quicksand may be escaped by slow movement of the legs in order to increase viscosity of the fluid, and rotation of the body so as to float in the supine position

With quicksand, the more you struggle in it the faster you will sink. If you just relax, your body will float in it because your body is less dense than the quicksand. If you step into quicksand, it won't suck you down. However, your movements will cause you to dig yourself deeper into it.

This got me thinking, sometimes in life I find myself struggling with the pressures of life, sin, etc., a storm may hit me, a test or trial may come and just like someone who has stepped into quicksand I panic, I thrash about, I try to dig myself out of the problem but only end up burying myself further. Instead of just relaxing in God and trusting in God that He will bring me through, deliver me, I struggle and sink.

In **Exodus 14:14 The LORD will fight for you; you need only to be still**

Be blessed today

Newbie

I remember when I first started going to Muntz St church; I had been away from church for a while and had been looking round for another church to go to but couldn't find one I was happy with. I don't know how I came to Muntz St; it is a church I have heard of before and had visited a couple times. However I went the one week and came back the next, after about say my 4th visit I spoke to the pastor there John Jackson, he asked me my plans and I said I wasn't sure, I just knew that I needed to be at a church otherwise I'd be lost back to the world, he advised me that in regards to a current situation that it is in my best interest that I remain coming and once I have sorted things out to let him know my plans. That was nearly 2 years ago, I got re-baptised and became a member. I didn't see that coming, which was definitely not in my plans, I remember speaking to him about it and he said it is not by accident that you are here, you are here amongst family, that's what you need, and that is what we offer amongst many other things.

What I'm saying is when it says in **Jeremiah 29:11 For I know the plans I have for you," declares the LORD, "plans to prosper you and not to harm you, plans to give you hope and a future and Isaiah 55:8-9 For my thoughts are not your thoughts, neither are your ways my ways," declares the LORD. For as the heavens are higher than the earth, so are my ways higher than your ways, and my thoughts than your thoughts.**

I would never have thought or planned to become a member of Muntz St, but it's a decision I most definitely do not regret.

Be blessed today as you are reassured that God knows the plan for each one of us and it will not harm us!

Backache

I've been having back ache for a week now and no signs of improving, I tried various medication but pain still there, so I tried to book an appointment with the doctor, I tried Tuesday only to be told no appointments, I tried to book one online, no appointment. I tried again this morning and after waiting 12 minutes on the phone I finally had to plead and managed to get an appt.

What came to me was that, sometimes when we need to speak with someone or get through to customer services etc. there's always at least 5 minutes of pressing 1 for this department, then pressing 5 for this and pressing 0 if you need to hear the options again, or to hear the message 'sorry our office is closed please call back again' but with Jesus, there isn't none of that, when I need to speak with Him there is no engaged tone, no hanging on for 10 minutes, no pressing of numbers to get put through to Him. All I need to do is call out to Him, He is never busy, never engaged, never closed. We have access to an omniscient, omnipresence and omnipotent God.

 Be blessed today as you take assurance God is never too busy to hear, answer and be there for you

Mirror Mirror

I have a few mirrors in my house and when I look into them they show back on outward reflection, if I have spots or blemishes it shows them, if I have grey hairs it will reflect that, if I have a dry spot on my face it will show me, it got me thinking, it's so easy to see an outward reflection but when it comes to inward reflection, that can be kind of hard. Apart from an x-ray how else can I see my inward self?

Yesterday we had a preacher from Nigeria called Pastor Joan Gamra and the message she preached on was the love of God/God's love.......not long after the preaching started you know when you begin to feel a bit uncomfortable in your seat and feel like the preacher is looking you dead in the eyes and preaching directly to you and about you, and you feel the whole church knows this? That's how I felt at certain points

Our theme for the ladies' weekend was grow in grace and I was speaking to my pastor in the morning about a situation and he said don't ask for more grace if you are not willing to use it (maybe not those exact words) and basically the same grace God bestows to me, who am I to not bestow it upon another, it's hard but I also believe it's not impossible. The preacher also said God demonstrated certain things to us, He didn't just say Michelle I love you, He demonstrated by sending His Son to die for me/us. I need to demonstrate grace to those who have offended/upset me.

2 Corinthians 13:5 says Examine yourselves to see whether you are in the faith; test yourselves. Do you not realize that Christ Jesus is in you--unless, of course, you fail the test? Self-examination is not easy but so vital, every now and then we detox our physical bodies from all toxins that are damaging us, I believe we need to also detox spiritually.

Be blessed as we examine what do we need to detox of today

Throwback

I was looking at a status I wrote about a year ago, and it was something the pastor's wife had said to me, she said I cannot speak life to others whilst I speak death to myself. That sentence really hit me, I like to encourage people, I like to write my blogs and I remember my pastor saying to me (during one of my down days) that I need to re-read what I have written, and I thought to myself nah its ok.

But it got me thinking, if someone came to me for example and said they felt suicidal and yes, I'm going to speak on a taboo topic because it's a real issue for people, I would encourage them of all that they have to live for, that what they are going through is just temporary, so why can't I speak life to myself when I feel suicidal.

If for example someone told me they felt unattractive/fat I would encourage them that nothing is wrong with them and not to listen to the small minded people and their opinions, and what we see on tv and magazines is not always a true reflection of how we are to look, so why can't I speak life to myself when I feel ugly and fat.

If someone is struggling spiritually, I would try and encourage them that they just need to hold on, that God loves them, and it may just be a trial they are going through, but they will come out the other side, so why can't I speak life to myself when I feel spiritually dead. In **Proverbs 18:21 Do not let any unwholesome talk come out of your mouths, but only what is helpful for building others up according to their needs, that it may benefit those who listen.**

Ephesians 4:29 The tongue has the power of life and death,
and those who love it will eat its fruit.

Be blessed today as we speak life to ourselves

Middle of the Night

I have a habit of waking up in the night or indeed the morning now the clocks went forward and stumbling around the landing using the walls as guidance because I can't be bothered to switch the light on, I've even encountered some cyclists riding along the road when its pitch black with no lights on and you can just about glimpse them.

Or sometimes I've gone into my attic looking for something and feeling around trying to guess the shape of what I've just grabbed, all because there is no light in there.

But on the flip side, sometimes when I'm driving some drivers have on their full beams so when I look in my rear view mirror, I am almost blinded, I can't help but know that they are there, their light alerts me to their presence.

Before I became a Christian I was stumbling along life in the dark, couldn't see clearly, couldn't think clearly, just like when I was on the landing and using the walls as a guide, I would use the wrong things to guide me.

Jesus said in **John 8:12 "I am the light of the world. Whoever follows me will not walk in darkness but will have the light of life."**

Too Good to be True

I saw this offer last week from a mobile provider and it seemed too good to be true, something like 20gb data and unlimited text and minutes a month for £12....well, I was sold, I had to have what they were offering, so I signed up with them and cancelling my old provider, they asked me why I was cancelling and I told them the offer to see if they could match it. They couldn't match it (which was no surprise) but he gave me more data and minutes than I had previously but for no less money, I said I might as well go with the other offer as for £12 a month I'm getting more, he then proceeded to advise me that they are the company that has the fastest 4g speed blah blah blah, so I thought about it and decided to stick with them.

It got me thinking, all these providers and broadband all offering something, some have fast speed, some offer mind-blowing deals, but the service is poor, all say they are the best, some tell you how great they are and what they can offer that nobody else can, but when it comes down to it, they don't deliver or it's not what you expected/signed up for. I could have got more data usage but the provider providing it I suppose wasn't one that really had a good track record for being reliable and so I changed my mind.

In the bible it tells us in **Isaiah 43:10 Ye are my witnesses, saith the LORD, and my servant whom I have chosen: that ye may know and believe me and understand that I am he: before me there was no God formed, neither shall there be after me.**

This tells me that there is no other God than God, none before Him and none after Him and whatsoever He says, He will do.

Be blessed today as you chose God as your provider

Looking Good

When it comes to washing and blow drying my hair, it must be pre planned, I can't just do it on the spur of the moment as its at least 2 to 3 hours of my time needed. The washing is not so bad, it's the drying, my hair shrinks, becomes knotty and halfway through the battle of trying to just come it out I'm ready to get the shaver and just shave it all off, no matter how much I prepare myself mentally, I always hit a clump of hair that is just stubborn and I'm ready to throw in the towel. So, now, I go to the hairdresser and make them fight the battle of my hair for me, my neighbour said to me once that I can wash my hair myself and I replied I know but I chose not to. It got me thinking, I could continue fighting my hair and getting stressed and wanting to resort to extreme measures or I could go to the hair dressers who have the patience, expertise and equipment to do it for me, and I suppose it's a bit like that when I am going through a battle in life, instead of trying to fight it by myself, in **2 Chronicles 20:15 - And he**

said, Hearken ye, all Judah, and ye inhabitants of Jerusalem, and thou king Jehoshaphat, Thus saith the LORD unto you, Be not afraid nor dismayed by reason of this great multitude; for the battle [is] not yours, but God's and in Exodus 14:14 The LORD will fight for you; you need only to be still.

This is saying to me that why am I fighting, I just need to be still, just like when I am approaching my hair with a comb I shouldn't be dismayed at the challenge ahead, God will fight my battle, I just need to give it to Him, if I don't give it to Him, I maybe could still win the battle but it may take me longer, may be more harder and may run into more difficulties.

Be blessed today as you let God fight the battle for you

Change

I was looking at the weather this morning and how it changed, when I left my house at 6.30am it was clear, by the time I looked out the window again it was foggy/misty, I couldn't see anywhere clear, I hadn't even seen the fog appear. Throughout the morning the fog/mist began to clear up.

It got me thinking, sometimes, well at lot of the time that is what it is like for me, one minute I'm ok and the next minute my whole outlook on life is foggy, I can't see ahead of me clearly, can't see my future clearly, it crept up on me slowly. I struggled to see what life had to offer me, I struggled to see Jesus, I struggled to see

In contrast what I could see was not what I needed to see; I saw a way out of the fog, but it wasn't by using my fog lights.

I shared something with my pastor today and a wave of fog covered me emotionally, but I'm trusting in that what I shared will allow the fog to clear and that I can stand on the scriptures below:

Psalm 119:105 says Your word is a lamp for my feet, a light on my path.

Ephesians 5:8 for you were formerly darkness, but now you are Light in the Lord; walk as children of Light

John 8:12 Then Jesus again spoke to them, saying, "I am the Light of the world; he who follows Me will not walk in the darkness, but will have the Light of life."

Be blessed today

Roses are?

I wrote a status in 2009 and it said if life is a bed of roses, why can I only feel the thorns?

I looked up the meaning of this saying and it said it means an easy and peaceful life. Most likely based on a rose, representing happiness and love. So, a bed of roses would represent a very happy life. I then looked at what are thorns and it said this: Thorns/prickles usually can't be broken off easily. ... Rose has prickles to protect themselves from predators

It then got me thinking, nowhere in the bible did it or does it say we will have an easy life; even the song goes "nobody told me the road would be easy". So, if I say why can I only feel the thorns/prickles, sometimes we need those thorns to protect us from what is out there, sometimes people may want to hurt/use/abuse us, sometimes we need protecting from our own emotions/family etc.

Roses are beautiful to look at, they smell nice and are usually given on valentine's day as a symbol of love, but as we have read the thorns are also a vital part of the plant's survival, the thorns may deter animals from climbing onto them and eating them, they may prevent us from picking them from someone's gardens as we don't want to get pricked.

Sometimes I detest my thorns in my life, but I believe they are the reason I am still here today; they have protected me from someone/something/situation, and they/I/we can't be easily broken.

Be blessed today as you rethink your thorns

Hope 1

This Christmas I hope to get a present, I hope to lose weight by Easter, I hope to go away on holiday, I hope to buy a new car, I hope to redecorate, I hope, I hope, I hope.

 Hope is described as a feeling of expectation and desire for a particular thing to happen or want something to happen or be the case. I looked on the internet and it said this... Biblical hope is the knowledge of facts, If someone says to you that "I hope you have a good day," there is no guarantee that the day will go well so is not a fact. A believer knows that their hope is solid, concrete evidence because it is grounded in the Word of God, and we know that God cannot lie.

 Romans 8:24-25 speaks of hope of something we do not have yet, it is based on something yet to come so we are in effect living in a state of hope daily, hope only ends when what we have hoped for has arrived.

1 Thessalonians 5:8 "But since we belong to the day, let us be self-controlled, putting on faith and love as a breast plate, and the hope of salvation as a helmet."

We have a hope that we will be with Jesus that He will return, to reign with Him, it has not happened yet, and it is a desire for it to happen, this is what keeps us,

RIP

This morning I woke up to hear the sad news that one of our members and sister in Christ had passed away, the news saddened me as I reflected on the person, always entering church singing and dancing and playing the tambourine at every opportunity. I spoke to my pastor and shared my feelings and he said although it is a time of mourning and grief it is also a time of rejoicing? I thought hang on a minute, someone has just died, but my pastor explained that our dear sis G as we fondly called her knew where she was going, she knew she was going home with the Lord, she had laboured tirelessly and worked hard evangelising to anyone and everyone, therefore we should rejoice because we know we will see her again, we can rest in the comfort of where her eternal home will be. It reminds me of the scriptures **John 11:23-26 Jesus said to her, "Your brother will rise again." Martha said to him, "I know that he will rise again in the resurrection on the last day." Jesus said to her, "I am the resurrection and the life**.

Whoever believes in me, though he die, yet shall he live, and everyone who lives and believes in me shall never die. Do you believe this?" and **Philippians 3:20-21** *But our citizenship is in heaven, and from it we await a Savior, the Lord Jesus Christ, who will transform our lowly body to be like his glorious body, by the power that enables him even to subject all things to himself.*

It just reminds me that death comes to us all, I don't know when, but it will come, but in the words of Matthew Henry

"He whose head is in heaven need not fear to put his feet into the grave."

Be blessed today, knowing that God will send His Comforter to us, to give us strength, hope and to wipe away our tears

Where o death is your victory, where o death is your sting

Hope 2

I have many periods throughout the year which I hate and become down and hate life, Christmas is one of them, all around I see families getting together around a large table full of food, fun, games and love, whilst I know that is a reality for some, I also realise it is also far from the truth for others, our theme for this month at church is hope, and to be honest, I feel hopeless. Pretty much like last year this Christmas I hope to get a present and then get disappointed as it was a desire or expectation of something.

I hope to lose weight by Easter, I hope to go away on holiday, I hope to buy a new car, I hope to redecorate, I hope my relationship with God is better in 2017, I hope, I hope, I hope.

 Hope is described as a feeling of expectation and desire for a particular thing to happen or want something to happen or be the case

I looked on the internet and it said this. Biblical hope is the knowledge of facts, if someone says to you that "I hope you have a good day," there is no guarantee that the day will go well so is not a fact. A believer knows that their hope is solid, concrete evidence because it is grounded in the Word of God, and we know that God cannot lie.

Rev Mark Letman said hope without faith is just a daydream, if I hope to have a better relationship with God then my faith needs to be the driving force, it's not going to happen by me just saying I hope, I need to do my part so that I am not just daydreaming. I hope to go to heaven, but what am I doing to make sure that it's just not a daydream, rev also said we can say to someone I hope you have a good day or hope you pass your driving test but there is no guarantee they will.

Romans 8:24-25 speaks of hope of something we do not have yet, it is based on something yet to come so we are in effect living in a state of hope daily, hope only ends when what we have hoped for has arrived. Be blessed today as we put our hope in God for, He will never fail us.

Christmas Time

It's that time of year again when I begin to feel dismayed, alone and discouraged, I'm trying to remain positive throughout this festive season but it's a battle I am losing rapidly. I know a lot of what they portray on TV is not reality but then again to a certain extent it is, there are going to be families all piled round the table laughing, joking, eating, sleeping and playing games, there are going to be those who are going to be eating maybe a tin of beans alone, there are going to be those on the streets hoping a kind stranger will buy them a sandwich, those who have no family, those who will be facing there first Christmas without a loved one, or in hospital with a sick relative/friend, each of us is going to experience this festive season in different ways, some happy, some sad, some situations beyond our control, others not so. It just reminds me that whilst I may not be having the Christmas, I see on TV what I do have is love, health, friends, family, roof over my head, food, money to buy food, heat, gas, water, clothes and so forth and there is somewhere I can go for Christmas day. So, I suppose as I write this, I'm trying to remind myself that life isn't perfect, there are no perfect scenarios, but all is not lost for me, I have more than many others and I am not saying that to boast, but as a reminder of the scripture in **Psalm 42:11 My spirit, why are you so sad? Why are you so upset deep down inside me? Put your hope in God. Once again, I will have reason to praise him. He is my Saviour and my God.**

Make-Up

I'm not really one to wear makeup, I wear it on occasions depending on what mood I'm in, sometimes I'll spend a lot of time putting it on, other times I do it in a hurry, sometimes I like how it looks, other times I don't.

It got me thinking, most days I smile, not always because I want to but because I have too, my smile is a bit like make up, I put make up it on in the morning and take it off a night, it covers my blemishes, makes my skin tone look even, etc., it hopefully makes my outer appearance pleasing to the eye.

I put my smile on in the morning for everyone to see and take it off once I get home, my smile covers the pain that I feel deep inside, it covers the hurt, the loneliness that I feel, if I smile then I am accepted by people as otherwise I usually get 'what you looking vex for, or, what have you got to be sad about'. If you don't smile, people tend to want to stay away from you.

However, I am fed up with having to smile when inside I'm dying.

Junk mail

Something my pastor mentioned on New Year's Day got me thinking, he spoke of us having to get rid of our junk. In my email I have a folder called junk and a folder called trash, in the junk folder this is where all random emails from 3rd parties go, they vary on subject such as I've won the lottery, so and so wants to meet me, compensation, job applications and the likes, and all I do is simply click 'empty folder' and they get sent to my trash or deleted folder, I don't even take the time to read them as I know its junk and it just clutters up my email.

It then got me thinking, I brought a new phone recently as my old one was struggling to get through the day without the battery dying, but before I had brought my new phone, my old one would have apps that run in the background, the minute I turned my phone on certain apps would spring to life and in the background be running and draining my battery and making my phone slower, I didn't know they were there and once I did I would have to go into each one to force it to stop. It's a bit like that in my life, I have a lot of 'apps' running in my mind, the minute I wake up things from the past, hurts, pains, anger, suicide and so forth begin to run in the background, and for the whole day they are there draining me out mentally and emotionally, make me lethargic, if I don't switch them off they will be there all day just running, doing nothing constructive except draining me. I need to be reminded of the scripture **Philippians 2:5 - Let this mind be in you, which was also in Christ Jesus**: this is the only 'app' I need running in the background daily.

Be blessed today as you clear out your junk mail

Open Sesame

I remember over the Christmas I rang my pastor in floods of tears and said I'm sick of being and feeling alone, and he replied the door was and is still open, but you have to choose to enter, and in my head, I was thinking but pastor you just don't understand. Anyway, I had a think about what he said, and it got me thinking, sometimes in my life I have knocked on doors with no answer, tried to open doors with no key or the wrong key, got locked out of doors as an unwanted guest. I remember watching Takeshi's Castle and there is this maze of doors that you have to go through, some of the doors you open lead to nowhere, some of the doors led to being chased by someone and some doors opened led you to falling in the water, however, there were also doors that if opened led you to the other side or to your goal.

Not every door I suppose is going to be open and not every open door is for me to enter, over the Christmas I choose to enter that door that was being opened and I felt at home, felt a part, yes it's difficult sometimes opening or entering a door but again my pastor said, if he didn't mean it, he wouldn't have said it, he was saying I have opened the door but I can't force you to enter, bit like the saying you can lead a horse to water but you can't make it drink.

It says in **Matthew 7:7-8 "Continue to ask and God will give to you. Continue to search, and you will find. Continue to knock, and the door will open for you. Yes, whoever continues to ask will receive. Whoever continues to look will find. And whoever continues to knock will have the door opened for them and John 10:9 I am the door: by me if any man enter in, he shall be saved, and shall go in and out, and find pasture.**

Be blessed today

Please Like

I'm not going to lie, there's times when I write a status, post a pic, or create a page and it doesn't attract a single like on Facebook, I mean, if I found that pic funny, why don't you, or why can't you like my page?

Then I look at what other people write and see how many 1000s of likes and shares their posts get, so, as you do, I get vexed.

But it got me thinking, a lot of the time when I write my posts I write for me, writing is my passion and sometimes I chose to share, other times I don't. I remember writing one particular thing on Facebook and not a single like or comment did it attract, but someone had said to me they had read it and it moved them, another person said to me that people on his friends list are seeing my posts and they enjoy it and it makes them asks questions.

So, if my status, poems, blogs, pics never get any more likes/comments is that a deciding factor if I should continue or not.... when Jesus was preaching there were some that would have received His word but made no comment, some would have questioned Him, and some may have shared what He said. However, even if no one commented, argued, agreed etc. Jesus would still have preached; it would not have stopped Him. I'm not comparing myself whatsoever but I'm reminding myself that someone liking my status does not give it validation or worth.

Be blessed today as you like and share my status....... only joking

Spot the Difference

A mirror reflects the outward appearance, it shows what you like, how your clothes look, if your hair and make-up is on fleek or not, what it does not show is your insides, an x-ray shows your internal body, your organs, your bones, it can show if there is something wrong, an x-ray for example can detect if a bone is broken, what it can't do is show the external body.

Some days I look in the mirror and physically I look fine, my hair is tidy, my clothes look good, but then, I take a minute to look at my x-ray and there is shows all my brokenness, no one can't see it because they don't have the equipment to see inside my body, my life, my emotions, sometimes I look at my x-ray and am surprised at what it shows as I didn't know it would show so much, sometimes it shows my ugliness, my hatred, my anger, my jealously.

Both mirrors and x-rays are important in my opinion, one cannot do the job of the other, sometimes I can spend all day looking in the mirror and marvel at the reflection whereas really, I should be looking at my x-ray and other days I spend so long looking at my inside I neglect to look at the outside. Today I smile, today my clothes look ok, but my x-ray is a different story, it paints a picture of brokenness, feels like every bone is broken and can't be mended. It's easier to look at the outward appearance as.

it is more visible, there are mirrors everywhere, but for an x-ray you need to book an appointment/go to hospital. Only trained people can take an x-ray and interpret it.

 It reminds me of the scriptures **Matthew 23:27-28 "Woe to you, scribes and Pharisees, hypocrites! For you are like whitewashed tombs which on the outside appear beautiful, but inside they are full of dead men's bones and all uncleanness. "So, you, too, outwardly appear righteous to men, but inwardly you are full of hypocrisy and lawlessness.**

 1 Samuel 16:7 But the LORD said to Samuel, "Do not look at his appearance or at the height

of his stature, because I have rejected him; for God sees not as man sees, for man looks at the outward appearance, but the LORD looks at the heart."

Be blessed today as we take assurance that God sees the x-ray of us, only He can fix what is broken, only He can mend a broken heart, only He can make us whole again.

The Book

I've heard the saying 'don't judge a book by its cover' and kind of agree with it, it says to me that based on the cover alone you can't determine how good the book will be, the cover could be colourful and enticing and once you open it, the story is lame, vulgar, disappointing or, the cover could be gloomy and dreary but once read it was one of the best books you have ever read!

Again, for example, I could go to someone's house and from the outside exterior I'm expecting great things for the interior, but, once I enter in the house has no carpet, settee and mould, again, I could buy a pineapple because it looks healthy but once I cut it, inside it's gone off.

I suppose what I'm saying is you can't look at an exterior of someone and determine their interior. Many times, I put on a smile, will laugh etc. but inside I'm dying, dying a slow death, but, because on the exterior I seem fine, people will assume my interior is fine, and, I know I have made the same assumption about other people.

Sometimes an exterior is needed in order to get by some people when selling cars will make the exterior appearance sparkling, but that could be to hide the fact that the interior has some defect/damage.

But what if we really showed our true exterior from the onset, would people still want to know us, be friends with us, how would we be treated. Sometimes I long to be true to myself but fear of reactions prevents me.

2 Corinthians 10:7You are looking at things as they are outwardly If anyone is confident in himself that he is Christ's, let him consider this again within himself, that just as he is Christ's, so also are we.

Baby

A new-born baby needs help, they cannot do anything for themselves apart from breathe, they cannot wash themselves, feed themselves, change their nappies, blow their nose, hold up their head, they can't speak to say what is wrong with them. They cry as a way of communication, they cry if they are hungry, in pain, tired or just want comfort, sometimes these cries can be different in terms of pitch.

As the baby gets older they need less help, after a while they can hold the bottle and eventually use cutlery to feed themselves, they can support their head, start crawling and eventually walk, they can indicate by words or actions if they are hungry etc. although they can now talk sometimes a cry is the best form of communication for them, maybe the child is frustrated and cannot put it into words so all they can do is cry.

Some people say when a baby cries that sometimes it is best to leave them to cry as if you run to them every time they cry then you are not helping them, if for example a baby is tired and they cry, instead of picking them up and rocking them, leave them until they cry themselves to sleep. I don't know if it's proven to be effective or not, but for me, as an adult I cry as a way of communicating, if I'm in pain, hurt or sad I cry, I don't want the theory of leave them to cry as they will cry themselves to sleep, I want to be attended to, to be comforted. There are some things I cannot put into words. It reminds me when it says in **Psalm 61:1-3 Hear my cry, O God; attend unto my prayer. From the end of the earth will I cry unto thee, when my heart is overwhelmed: lead me to the rock that is higher than I. For thou hast been a shelter for me, and a strong tower from the enemy.**

Be blessed today

Money Money

When my son was younger, he didn't appreciate the value of the money he had or the value of something I brought him, i.e., pair of jeans etc., to him it was just a pair of jeans or a pair of trainers, no thought process into maybe I had to sacrifice a bill or spending that money may leave me a bit short. It meant nothing to him. But now that my son is older and beginning to buy things for himself, he is appreciating the value of money, still not as much as I do as he has no outgoings as such.

 It got me thinking, many a time I don't appreciate the value of having God within me, in my life, before me and beside me, I don't value what God can do, not only in terms of blessings but also in terms of protection, Him being my strength, my support, as I grow older in the faith surely I should begin to value this more than I did in the beginning but somehow I fall short. What will it take for me to value God, to value that when He says no weapon formed against me shall prosper? to value that I am the head and not the tail, that I am blessed and highly favoured.

Today I feel down, today I feel detached from it all, today I hardly know who I am, today I need to detach my feelings from my faith, my faith should be there regardless of how I feel, I should value my faith, value my relationship with God. I don't even know where this blog is going but I speak to myself more than anyone else today.

Be blessed, recognise and value who God is and in you

Clogged Up

I have what they call a 'bagless vacuum', I prefer these types because it's a lot cheaper than having to find the correct vacuum bags and then buy them, however, what I noticed along the years that although its bagless, it still needs to be emptied from time to time. There was an occasion when I was vacuuming and wondering why there were bits still left on the floor, when I checked, its suction power was reduced because it was clogged up, it needed emptying, another occasion I was vacuuming and it just switched off, it overheated due to it being clogged, and the safety mechanism cut in, another time I was vacuuming and sucking up everything in sight, even things that I shouldn't really be vacuuming up.

 It then got me thinking, sometimes my life/emotions is like a vacuum, I keep picking up stuff that I don't need to, become clogged emotionally/mentally, and need to be emptied, other times I am so clogged up I become less effective as a person, as a child of God, I am too full up of rubbish that I have no room for anything else, I pick up everything in sight, other times I become so clogged up I shut down mentally and emotionally, I switch off from everything and everyone, I no longer work.

This year I face a big challenge, I need to empty my 'vacuum' of baggage, of rubbish, of hurts, rejections, painful memories etc., it's a hard challenge but I know it's a challenge that is vital for me to be effective, to be who God created/desired me to be. I cannot be a clogged-up vacuum no more.

In the words of **William Murphy 'empty me empty me empty me, God if you find anything that's not like you I want you to take it away, when you search my heart God if you find anything that's not like you Take it away, empty me empty me yeah fill won't you fill me with You'.**

Consequences

 I was watching Emmerdale and Coronation St a few weeks back and in Emmerdale one of the characters was pushed off a bridge trying to escape his partner, he landed on a car, this car's airbag then inflated, restricted the drivers view and caused the car to crash, an oncoming car then crashed into that car and eventually caused a pile up. In Coronation St one of the characters was seeking revenge on someone and sped off in his car, he didn't see his daughter in the road, swerved to avoid her, the car overturned and resulted in someone being burnt.

 What came to me was this, one person's action can have devastating consequences for other people, when we gossip for example, are we damaging another person. Over the years people have said things to me, done things to me, and in response my actions have then affected someone else, for example if someone over the years constantly lies to me, if I then develop a new friendship, I may push that person away for fear of them also lying to me. We don't always know that our actions can have devastating consequences, when someone is being bullied, a consequence of that can be that the victim kills themselves, if someone is abused whether mentally, physically, or emotionally, sometimes that person goes on to abuse others.

The definition of consequence is defined as a result of a particular action or situation, often one that is bad or not convenient.

As a consequence of Adam and Eve's actions Jesus suffered on the cross, He was rejected, ridiculed, unwanted.

There are consequences for us all according to **Romans 3:23 - For all have sinned, and come short of the glory of God,** the key word is 'all', it's not saying some have fallen short, but we all have and the consequences further are found in **Romans 6:23 - For the wages of sin [is] death; but the gift of God [is] eternal life through Jesus Christ our Lord.**

Cry

There is a chorus that goes 'hear my cry oh Lord and attend unto my prayer' and then there is another chorus that goes weeping may endure for a night, but joy comes in the morning'.

I often wonder how long is a' night' and when does the 'morning' come, usually a night is the period between sunset and sunrise and morning is the period between midnight and noon. So logically weeping will endure for one night and joy will immediately follow in the morning? But in **2 Peter 3: 8 it says, 'but do not forget this one thing, dear friends: With the Lord a day is like a thousand years, and a thousand years are like a day'.**

 It says on the internet that time is the condition of man's thought and action, but not of God's. His thoughts are not as our thoughts, nor His ways as our ways; what seems a delay to us is none to Him. What I understand from this that a night and a morning is not meant in the way in which we seem, there's nothing to say that my joy won't come in the morning, but what if my morning is in 2 weeks' time or 6 months' time. God know us all individually and to everything there is a time, a time to cry, a time to die etc., a time to weep and a time for joy. It all happens in time. Just not maybe our time. The other chorus is us having a conversation with God, we are asking Him to listen and are expecting Him to answer, we are asking Him to hear our cry, not to see it, but to hear it and to attend to us, sometimes when a child cries and we see they are crying but ignore them, they cry even louder so that we notice and so that we attend to them, God is our father, our Abba father and although he sees our tears sometimes He wants us to cry out to Him, to reach out to Him, saying Abba Father I need you.

Be blessed today

Thief in the Night

About 7 years ago I got broke into, I was asleep at the time, but something made me wake up and as I woke up the thief was in my bedroom, he reached over and grabbed my phone and told me not to say anything and ran down the stairs, without thinking I immediately got out my bed and ran down the stairs after him, when I looked out my front door there were a couple others with him and they laughed as they ran on.

I was annoyed and angry at myself for sleeping through it, how could I not hear the door being kicked in, then I was angry at the audacity of the thief because he knew I was in my room as my TV was on, you could hear the sound and see the light reflecting, but he still chose to enter.

 What came to me was that the thief was looking for something, he didn't just break in for the sake of it, he had hoped to come away with something of value. The devil breaks in, he breaks into my life and tries to steal my joy, my peace, my happiness, my mind, my hope, my future, and just like I never heard the thief break in and enter, sometimes I don't see/hear/feel the devil breaking in until it's too late, he is already there, but instead of chasing him out, I offer him residence, a place of rest. If I can chase a thief who only steals material things, how much more should I chase a thief that is trying to steal spiritual and emotional things?

John 10:10 says the thief comes only to steal and kill and destroy; I have come that they may have life and have it to the full. The devil knows that greater is He that is in us than he that is in the world, he knows we have value, are valuable and so he wants us, but God wants us more and in **James 4: 7** we are told to **submit yourselves to God. Resist the devil, and he will flee from you.**"

Be blessed today

I do

When we meet someone deep down we long for that relationship to develop into marriage, we get to know that person, we spend time with them, learning about them and all their good bits and ugly bits, we want to be with that person forever, we love them and don't want to lose them, when we get married we make vows, we say for better or for worse, for richer or poorer, in sickness and in health, we are making a vow that come what may I will still love you, if I'm broke, if you're sick, I will love you, if we argue, if we fall out, I will still love you, I will not let anything or anyone come between us or separate us. The same applies to God, when we get baptized we make a promise to God that no matter what we will serve him, if I'm broke I will love him, if I'm sick I will love him, if nothing is going my way I will love him, when things are good I will love him, we will not allow anything to come between us and God, when we have a relationship with God, like any other relationship we need to get to know God, spend time with him, show him our good bits and our most shameful bits, to want to be with him daily, to know more about him. God wants a relationship with us, he wants to know that in sickness and health, better or worse, richer or poorer nothing will separate us from the love of God. Romans 8:31-39

I'm so in Love

In 2 days' time, there are going to be loads of loved up couples sending and receiving cards, buying a multitude of roses, proposing, going out for romantic meals, getting married, and also on that day there are going to be loads of people feeling unloved, alone, wondering why nobody is there valentine, let's face it, February 14th is all about love, it got me thinking, I suppose deep down i would like to be a part of that day, to wake up and watch my loved one open his card/present, to be in suspense as to what gift he may have brought me and then spend the day working out what I'm going to wear for our candlelight romantic dinner. however, valentine's day is going to be like any other ordinary day for me, it got me thinking, just because I don't have a valentine to buy for doesn't mean I'm unloved or not wanted, it doesn't mean I will never get to spend a valentine's day with someone, it's all in God's time, and does valentine day really mean anything anyway apart from spending money and declaring undying love. the truth is, we all have a valentine on February 14th and every other day to be honest, in **Deuteronomy 4:24 it says, "For the LORD your God is a consuming fire, a jealous God",** whether we are single, engaged, married, entertaining, above all and everyone we are to love God first. Above your wife, husband, girlfriend, boyfriend, children, God loves us, He paid the price for us, He brought us, and He is my valentine.

Wait

I'm a very impatient person, punctuality is one of my strong points and I get a bit frustrated when people are late, if we agree to meet at 10am and 10.01 you haven't arrived, I'm calling you to see where you are. I hate waiting for buses, for dinner to cook when I'm hungry, if my hair appointment runs over the expected finish time, I don't like to wait! I remember a while back I was stuck in traffic, and I was getting frustrated and decided to take a short cut because I simply couldn't wait in the queue, needless to say, that short cut probably added an extra 40 minutes to my journey because everyone was taking that short cut and it created an even longer queue. If I tell my son to turn off something and 2 minutes later, it's still on. I shout because I don't understand why it's not done straight away. I suppose what I'm saying really is, is that there's times I'm waiting on the lord, and He is not showing up, I'm waiting for my healing and it's not coming, I'm waiting for my husband and I can't see him, I'm waiting, but waiting very impatiently, and sometimes try to rush it or take a short cut.

Abraham – The Father of Many Nations- took years of waiting for a child
Joseph- waited to be the leader of his people
Job- lost everything but waited on God to reveal His plan
Simeon- waited for the Messiah

The above people waited but however, there are consequences on not waiting on God
Abraham stopped
waiting. He had a son by another woman. This ultimately caused him many problems

Be blessed today as we remember **Psalm 27:14 Wait for the LORD; Be strong and let your heart take courage; Yes, wait for the LORD.**

Impatience

I'm the kind of person that when buying something I do one of two things, if it's an electrical item, or something that needs assembling, I tend to ignore the instructions, press loads of buttons and hope for the best, and, after a frustrating hour or so I have to resort to the instructions or manual or, if it's an item of clothing I examine the care label so I know whether its dry clean, made of wool, what temperature to wash it etc. the reason being is I don't want to ruin or spoil what I have just purchased and it got me thinking, the bible is in a way our manual/instruction booklet in how to live right, how to care of ourselves, we were brought with a price (Jesus dying) and God want to make sure that we don't spoil or ruin so we are giving the word. However, if like me in the first example we don't bother to read the word and just hope for the best, the end result is not going to be how it should be, most times I have pieces of wood or screws left over or a piece of shelving in the wrong place, so I need to dismantle and start over. I also got thinking that in a financial transaction there's two things an action (picking up the item and taking it to the checkout) and an answer/response (our money being accepted). The chorus that comes to mind is I am redeemed, brought with a price, so, the financial transaction there is us being redeemed and the response is we were brought with a price. Other examples of action and answers/responses are in the Lord's prayer we say forgive us (action) as we forgive others (answer), we are told to ask (action) and it shall be given (answer), knock (action) and it shall be opened (answer), we are told to come unto Jesus (action) and he will give us rest (answer).

Fenced In

This morning I was walking to work and there is an unused car park which had been fenced up to stop people from parking there, I'd say over the last 3 months or so since it's been unused, they have to come out and re-fence the car park due to vandalism. I took a picture of it this morning, one pic shows where the fence has been knocked down and the other pic where the fence is how it should be. Then it got me thinking and this chorus came to mind 'Jesus be a fence all around me every day, Lord, I want you to protect me as I travel along the way'.

The definition of a fence is Noun: a barrier, railing, or other upright structure, typically of wood or wire, enclosing an area of ground to prevent or control access or escape. Verb: surround or protect with a fence and archaic: a means of protection.

 When we are asking Jesus to be a fence around us my opinion is that we want protection, we don't want anything to get in and harm us, don't want anyone to rob us, damage our property, sometimes a garden will have a fence and that is to separate the two gardens and maybe offer some privacy, to let you know that this section is your garden, or shepherds may fence their sheep in the field to stop the wolves from eating them. When I sing that chorus, I want Jesus to protect me from danger such as being attacked, being in an accident, from people who would want to hurt me, I want Him to barricade Himself around me, around my thoughts, around my actions.

Lamentations 3:7 says God built a fence around me that I cannot climb over, and he chained me down.
I want God to fence me in so much that I can't climb over Him, and nothing can climb over Him.

Be blessed today as you let Jesus be a fence around you

Eye Spy

Yesterday I went for an eye test, it was about 3 years overdue, but I didn't want to pay full price for a test, a colleague at work gave me a voucher for a half price eye test, kept it in my bag for a couple of months and then finally decided to use it, because as far as I am concerned nothing is wrong with my eyesight. They done an initial check on my eyes and one of the checks I had to stare at a green light and this machine would move around trying to locate possibly my iris/pupil...something to do with my eye, anyway it then proceeded to take photos of the back of my eye and blow some air into it (have no idea what the air was for).

Long story short after doing various tests they discovered I have a white shadow on my optic nerve and requires further tests but also that my near sight vision has gotten worse (weren't impressed). Whilst I was there, I also booked myself for a free hearing test. It got me thinking that my near vision is not so good, so sometimes

I see things a bit blurry or need glasses to help take the strain off my eyes, sometimes in life my near vision is not good either as sometimes I fail to see what is in front of me or fail to acknowledge the blessings I have, fail to see the people who are in my life but have no problem seeing the people who aren't.

I wouldn't have known about the white shadow on my optic nerve as it is not visible to the human eye and the optician was surprised it hadn't been noticed before as it had possibly been there since birth. Again, it got me thinking of the scripture **1 Corinthians 2:9 says However, as it is written: "What no eye has seen, what no ear has heard, and what no human mind has conceived" -- the things God has prepared for those who love him—**

Sometimes we fail to see or hear from God because we are not tuned in to Him or keeping our eyes on Him. Sometimes we need to take a spiritual eye check to make sure we have not lost sight of who God is, where is has brought us from and where He will lead us.

On Guard

I was walking to town yesterday and as I was walking I noticed this cat being very still, its eyes were firmly fixed straight ahead, its body poised and ever so slowly it crept forward, every now and then it would stop so as not to make a noise, eyes still firmly fixed straight ahead, I was watching in amazement and noticed that the cat was actually watching a pigeon on the ground pecking away for food, the pigeon had no idea the cat was there or that the cat was watching him and creeping up on him, the cat, however, knew its prey and was doing all it could to creep up on him, as I approached the cat it turned its gaze to me, but still kept its body poised in position should it need to pounce on the pigeon and then turned its eye back to the pigeon.

It got me thinking, sometimes, the devil sneaks up on us, it sees its prey (us) and just like the cat it sneaks up slowly on us, ready to pounce at the right time, we, like the pigeon are going about our daily life and can't see or hear the cat, we are unaware of the impending danger, the devil doesn't take its eye of us and is poised to attack right when we least expect it. May not be a physical attack, may be attack of the mind, the emotions,

1 Peter 5:8 says be sober, be vigilant; because your adversary the devil, as a roaring lion, walketh about, seeking whom he may devour:

We don't know when the enemy is going to attack us, this last couple of weeks has been very difficult for me, I've retreated into myself and no longer smile or laugh like how I used to, my mind is fixed on one thing and it's not a positive thing, that's why in the instruction given in the following scripture should be heeded to, I haven't and I'm paying the price!

Ephesians 6:11: "Put on the whole armour of God that you may be able to stand against the schemes of the devil."

Bible Study

Last week was bible study and it was looking at **Romans 12- where it said be ye transformed by the renewing of your mind.** However, I have been going through some stuff so I told my pastor I am not coming, how can I transform my mind when I barely understand it. On Sunday morning pastor preached again on the same topic and I was vexed, it felt like he was talking to me, I already tried to escape it once and here I am now having to listen to it, but you know what, I believe that my pastor repeated the same thing on Sunday because it was meant for me to hear (pastor said that he doesn't usually preach what he discusses in bible study as he likes to keep them separate).

I looked at the word transformed in the dictionary, and it says to change completely the appearance or character of something or someone, especially so that that thing or person is improved: to change in character or condition.

So, when it tells me in **Romans 12 Do not conform to the pattern of this world but be transformed by the renewing of your mind.** Then you will be able to test and approve what God's will is--his good, pleasing and perfect will.

What it is telling me that my current mind set and if I am to be honest with you is one of self-destruction is not good, it is not the will of God for me to be in self-destruct mode all the time, God is telling me that there is room for improvement, I am not perfect, never will be, but I can be improved, my mind can be improved so that instead of thinking of death, I need to transform it to a better condition and think of life, I need to change the character and outlook of my future, instead of thinking I have no future, I have no hope, I have no purpose, I need to transform it and say my future is going to be good, may not have all the things I want but I will have all I need.

I'm not going to lie and say that's it's easy for me to transform my mind, I am having great difficulty, imagine, if for years someone repeatedly tells you that you are stupid an no good, then you will grow up believing it, so much so, that when someone comes along and tells you that actually you are good, it's hard for you to get your head around because all you've known is that you're stupid.

I believe God does not ask us to do anything impossible as that would be setting us to fail and God is not a man that He should lie, God knows we have it in us to transform our minds, we/I just have to believe that we have it in ourselves too, transforming your mind is achievable, not necessarily easy, not necessarily overnight, not necessarily permanent as we all revert back time to time, but to grow in God I need to transform my mind.

What did you say?

On Monday I went for a hearing test, it was
being done for free, so I thought why not? And
in the build up to the appointment I was
convinced my hearing was bad.
The audiologist asked me a few questions and
then took me to the booth to begin the test; he
put two ear buds in my ear and told me to click
every time I heard a sound.
Some of the sounds were quite loud, some were
low, and some were just about audible and
there were times I thought I heard a sound so
clicked anyway.
Anyway, my hearing was quite good and don't
need to go back for another 5 years but what
got to me was this:
 I had to concentrate in order to hear the sound,
sometimes it was so faint I even doubted myself
that I had heard it, sometimes when God speaks
to us it can be a loud sound, sometimes it can
be quiet and maybe sometimes faint, if I didn't
concentrate and focus my mind I would have

missed some sounds and then be told my hearing was poor.

Sometimes God has spoken to me but because I've not being concentrating or focusing on hearing His voice I've missed it, and then, like the times when I clicked the button because I thought I heard a sound, I think I hear God's voice and act upon it (usually when it's because I want to convince myself I heard from God so I can do whatever it is my heart was set upon).

John 10:27 says 'my sheep hear my voice, and I know them, and they follow me.

It's important that we know its God speaking to us and not any other contrary spirit.

Be blessed today as we hear Gods voice

Repairable

I saw a status this morning and it got me thinking; remember the nursery rhyme humpty dumpty and that after he fell no one could put him back together again?

There are many of us who are broken, who come to God broken, who walk around living a broken life, most days I feel broken, I feel like I've been smashed into a thousand pieces and none of the pieces can be superglued together again. In order to be fixed you need to be broken in the first place, that could be mentally, physically, emotionally or spiritually. I long for the day when I will be whole. I've been broken for more years than I care to think about. Sometimes we go to the wrong people in order to get fixed or turn to the wrong things thinking they will fix us. In the nursery rhyme it said that all the kings' horses and all the kings' men couldn't put humpty back together again. It doesn't say how many horses and kings' men but

I would imagine it was in the thousands. What is hindering us from being fixed?

But we have a king that can put us back together again, in **Jeremiah 17:14 it says God, pick up the pieces. Put me back together again. You are my praise!**

I had an item that had a piece come away and I used some superglue to try and fix it, but the glue wasn't strong enough to fix it, I had to get the right strength glue! God wants to put us back together again, I know He is desperate to fix me, but to be honest, I'm fighting against Him. I want to be fixed but I don't want to acknowledge the broken pieces in order to be fixed

Be blessed today as we think of the song that says the potter wants to put you back together again, oh, the potter wants to put you back together again

Round 1

I'm not really into boxing but take for example a fight to see who the next heavy weight becomes champion. In order to even consider being a champion you need to know your opponent, you will probably do some research on them; see how much they weigh, how much fights they have won, lost etc. and if it's by knockout. You will maybe try to identify any weaknesses they have and look at previous fights to get an idea of their fighting style. Also, when preparing for a fight they match opponents against weight so for example a featherweight wouldn't fight a heavyweight.

You may even begin a strict training regime so that you don't tire out easily, you need to be able to endure to the end, you will also need to eat the correct foods i.e., white meat, vegetables, and fruit to maintain your weight so that you can fight.

As Christians we fight daily, I know personally I'm always in a fight, but I don't always prepare myself to win. In Ephesians 6 v 13 we are told how to prepare ourselves to win the fight and by reading, praying and knowing who our enemy is, if you don't know who your enemy is it is hard to prepare to fight. We need to learn how to block punches the devil tries to throw at us.

But we are also told in **Ephesians 6 v 12 that we wrestle not against flesh and blood**, so we can't prepare ourselves for the fight by eating the right foods or by training.

Bad

I remember talking to someone and telling them I was 'a bad and a wicked person' and they were asking for evidence to support what I was saying, so I showed them what was written in black and white, and their response was that is just an indication of bad behaviour.

According to the dictionary behaviour is described as the way in which one acts or conducts oneself, especially towards others whereas the character of a person is defined as the mental and moral qualities distinctive to an individual.

The person was trying to tell me that although my behaviour may have been bad because I conducted myself in a bad way, it doesn't mean I am a bad person. If a person for example has had a lot of traumas whether in childhood or adulthood, or if a person is hurting so deeply, a way of expressing that pain and hurt may be through behaviour, they may go out and shop lift, indulge in drugs, have eating disorders, that doesn't render them a bad person, just a person trying to express whether knowingly or unknowingly their pain.

It got me thinking, if I keep thinking my behaviour is who I am, I am forever going to believe I am bad, but if I can begin to slowly separate the two and realise that I am a person dealing with great trauma from the age of 5 months old then perhaps the healing process can start to begin. I can't begin it if my mind-set still says and thinks I'm bad. I have been challenged to say my behaviour does not define who I am. My behaviour is saying I am hurt, I am broken. I need to be fixed

Candy

I'm a fan of candy crush and get obsessed with trying to finish the level so I can move on to the next one, I get excited thinking what challenges the next level will give me, when I get stuck on a level I get a bit frustrated that I have to remain on that level for sometimes a week or more and the smile that comes on my face when I finally finish the level is massive.

It got me thinking, as a Christian I am not to remain on the same level I am with God, there are higher heights and deeper depths for me to reach, just like candy crush, I should be aiming to move to the next level, sometimes I need to remain where I am for period but not permanent, I need to move to a next level in my worship, in my bible study, my prayer, my relationship with God. Just like when at school we don't stay on the same level mathematics book for the entire 5 years at school, the teachers aim is to progress us on to the next level, in martial arts or boxing you aim to move up to the next belt or weight. To move to the next level in a sport for example can be difficult, may require extra training, new routines, more dedication, a desire and determination. I don't believe God wants us to remain at the same level spiritually for our whole Christian walk; there are many scriptures about growing.

Sometimes in our jobs we desire to move to the next pay grade or seek promotion, there are many examples I could give about moving to the next level.
It makes me look at myself and reflect on have I moved up a level or have I indeed moved down a level, what am I doing to move up to the next level in my faith

There is a song that goes' **just take me to the next level in you, I wanna climb, there's new water, there's new wine, I'm ready to go forward, please take me to the next place, the**

higher place, just take me to the next level in you'

Be blessed today.

Practicality

Over the years I've prayed to God for various things, i.e., new job, bigger house, husband etc. But not always receiving, and then I've also seen other people praying AND receiving. I'm like whoa, what's going on here, so I'll pray again and still nothing.

I was reading romans 4 verses 18-22 yesterday and it was speaking about the promise God made to Abraham that he would be the father of many nations, bearing in mind Abraham was old and maybe not in the era of when Viagra was made, and his wife was barren. To be truthful I've read that scripture many times but not thought much of it, but the commentary said the following …. Isaac was born via Immaculate Conception but by a miracle conception. Abraham still had his part to play, he still had to have sexual relations in order to even start the conceiving process, BUT he done it believing. Sarah had to have faith that her barren womb would no longer be barren. FAITH is what was needed and what they had.

If I am honest, I had never thought about it like that, I just imagined poof, there's the baby. It really got me thinking about how important faith in God is and what part we must play, if Abraham just waited without action, there would be no Isaac, Abraham had the kind of faith mentioned in Hebrews 11:1 'now faith is the substance of things hoped for, the evidence if things not seen.
 So if I pray to God or if God has promised me something, I need to look at what am I doing, am I being proactive if I pray for a new job, am I looking for a job, applying for jobs, touching up my skills or am I just sitting there, sometimes jobs can come without effort put in to it but on the whole there is an action on our part, if I pray for a husband, what am I doing, am I preparing myself mentally and emotionally, am I being sociable, am I actively seeking or I am stuck in my house day after day with no contact with the

outside world. It just reminded me that you cannot be hungry and expect the food to just magic its way from the fridge to our mouths.

Missing Piece

Have you ever had a jigsaw puzzle and you get
to the end and there is one piece left, it looks
like it's the right piece, has the right
colour/picture, right size but try as you may the
piece just won't fit in, you squash it, you bang it,
you force it until the piece then starts to bend,
you eventually make it fit but alas, it's just not
the right piece.

Sunday I was at church and had to leave my
seat to go in the toilets and just breakdown, I
had looked around earlier and this never ending
journey of belonging just got too much, I felt like
I was that last piece of jigsaw forcing myself into
households, trying to fit into households, but
I'm just not the right piece, it made me realise
that no matter what I will never be the right
piece, the household I'm trying to fit into
already has their jigsaw complete with the right
pieces. Or sometimes when you see a parking
space and you think yes, my car can fit in there

so you start the manoeuvre, only to discover the gap is just not big enough, but from afar it looked it, again on my journey of belonging that's how it feels, that there may be a space for me but you try to manoeuvre in there and you realise the space is not big enough. It's a hard journey and many don't understand, many moan at me, but unless you have experienced a desire to belong then I must try to understand why you don't understand, it's a desire that sometimes I can't control, bit like when you're desperate for the toilet, you can only hold it for so long before the desire becomes unstoppable. I tried to look at the scripture where it says God is a father to the fatherless and if your mother or father forsake you as a source of comfort, but I admit it's a struggle.

Plants

I'm not very green fingered but I'll give it a try
and have a few plants that I try to take care off,
over time I've picked up tips to help plants grow
such as removing dead leaves/flowers, use plant
food to promote growth and to water
sometimes more when the weather is hot,
yesterday I came home and one of my plants in
the nagging basket had drooped over the edges
and hanging limp, I watered the plant and over
the course of the next few hours it 'came back
to life' and no longer drooped or hung limp.

The physical appearance of the plant alerted
me to the fact that it needed watering, it was
dying, wasn't going to last much longer, it
needed its life source. Over the past few weeks
spiritually I have drooped, I am hanging limp, I
needed water, I was running dry and dying, I
wasn't removing dead things to help promote
growth, my life source was not fed to me by me,
I wasn't watering my spirit with spiritual food, I
wasn't watering more than I should have

when I was parched, I neglected to water and just like plants, after a while they die.

There is contraption that allows plants to be drip fed each day so that they are always watered and the scripture below kind of reminds me of this, to never thirst again the key thing is I need to drink, not tap water, or mineral water or spring water but the water that spring up eternal life, but if I don't drink, I will thirst

John 4:14 says but whoever drinks of the water that I will give him shall never thirst, but the water that I will give him will become in him a well of water springing up to eternal life

Be blessed today

Hide n Seek

Have you ever played the game hide and seek
where a group of people hide and someone
then has to find them, I played it a few times as
a child and you prayed you wouldn't be found,
some people then grow out of childhood games,
but it seems that I'm still playing it, I'm hiding
from God and praying He won't seek me. I try to
hide because I am ashamed, because I've
messed up again, because I think God doesn't
love me no more.

I remember once I was playing hide and seek
and because I chose a good hiding place, the
person seeking me gave up looking for me and
left me where I was in the dark wardrobe. God
doesn't give up on me, He doesn't say ok, I'm
tired, He doesn't leave me in my hiding place,
my dark dreary hiding place, He seeks me out.

Adam and Jonah tried to hide from God, both in
different ways, Adam tried to hide in the Garden

of Eden but even though God asked Adam where he was, God knew.

 Jonah tried to hide/run from God to another city, do we not know that God is omnipresent, if we go to Spain; God is there, if we go Timbuctoo, God is there. This week I've been hiding, desperate not to be found and I need to remind myself of the scripture below

Jeremiah 23:24 "Can a man hide himself in hiding places, so I do not see him?" declares the LORD "Do I not fill the heavens and the earth?" declares the LORD.

Labour

I used to watch a programmes called on born
every minute, special delivery and labour ward
(I think) anyway, as you can gather from the
titles it all about childbirth, my own labour
lasted 26 hours and I know there are some
people whose labour lasted 4 hours, some
lasted days and for some 20 minutes, no one
can predict how long our labour will be, how
long it will take the baby to travel down the
birth canal, I wish there was a way lol and I
wished that when I was going through my own
labour that there was something I could do to
hurry it along, 26 hours of pain, of cramps, of
aches, of thinking I can't take one more
contraction, of being physically and mentally
drained and tired, all the energy going out of me
(which evidently was needed for the final PUSH
stage of labour)

 The same can be said when we are going
through life, hurt, pains, trials. I'm going through
labour right now, not in the physical

sense, I have hurts, pains, rejection, my past that I am having to push my way through to birth a new me, a new life, it's painful, gas and air aren't really helping and although I may take medication to numb the pain, like all medication it wears off and the pain is stronger than before. But one thing with labour…. eventually it will lead to delivery, regardless of how long you have been having contractions, eventually the sign we have been waiting for…. the urge to push comes and new life is birthed. I have been in labour for 20

years but I know each contraction is pushing me towards new life, towards my birth canal where I will emerge a new me.

Sometimes the pain is so much I cry out, begging for the pain to stop but I'm reminded of the following scripture **John 16:21 "Whenever a woman is in labour she has pain, because her hour has come; but when she gives birth to the child, she no longer remembers the anguish because of the joy that a child has been born into the world.**

Be blessed as we remind ourselves no pain, no gain. Labour is not forever

Beautiful

There's been a few times where I have cooked dinner and it looks just lovely and I'm dying to show it to the world, or maybe an artist or designer has created something and they are so proud of it everyone needs to see it, they want to show it off, every time they look at it their heart beams with pride, they created something so beautiful they just keep looking at it. That is how Gods is to us, there is a song by Tasha Cobbs, and it goes 'He said, you are beautiful my lovely creation can't take my eyes off you'

Although we may look at ourselves a different way, we may not feel beautiful, may not feel something to be proud of, but just imagine after a long anticipated 9 months of pregnancy you have just given birth to your baby and the baby is handed to you, you can't take your eyes off the baby, soaking in every detail, beaming with pride that you have created such a beautiful human being, again, that is how God looks at us, despite our blemishes, sins, mistakes etc. God is saying you are beautiful, my lovely creation.

Be blessed today

The Door

From an early age I have heard the saying 'you born in a barn', whenever I entered a room, meaning that when I open a door I need to close it behind me, a practice I still try and do today. On the opposite hand my son closes every door behind him and I have to ask to open it, however, there have been some doors that have been opened to me and after I have entered I close it, but these particular doors are not meant to be closed, for in closing then I am locking myself out, in closing them I am restricting my access, in closing them I am on my own. Sometimes I don't even realize that I've closed the door and other times I've closed the door because I fear rejection or abandonment so it's better for me to close it first before it's closed for me. I remember once I closed my living room door and it became jammed as the wood had warped and I had to kick it in so that I could gain access again, that took a lot of effort and force and broke part of the door. I don't

want to keep locking myself out from people
and then find that I have to kick my way back in.

My pastor asked me last week 'who had closed
the door' meaning the door he had opened
hadn't and hasn't been closed by him.

I'm having to learn that I don't always need to
close every door that is open to me. It's hard a
fear or flight kicks in, but, if people open their
door to me in the first place, then they must
want me to enter in.

Guilty by association

 I was watching a drama maybe sometime last year and basically someone got arrested and jailed because of a new law called guilty by association, the person hadn't committed a crime, didn't even know a crime was going to be committed, but, because he was there, he was found guilty! To some this may sound an injustice; he was innocent so why should he be treated as though he was guilty?

This got me thinking, I was reading Romans chapter 5 yesterday from verse 9 onwards and just like the scenario above, we all are guilty by association and have been sentenced. You may be thinking how? Well, the commentary for the scripture I was reading said this... Adam is the common father of every person on the earth; every human who has ever lived was "in" Adam's genetic makeup. Therefore, all mankind sinned in Adam; Humans are mortal - subject to death - before they commit any sin themselves. Since mortality is the result of sin, it shows that we are made sinners by Adam's sin, not by our own personal sin.

Even a new-born baby is a sinner even though they have not even had the chance to commit a sin. But there is hope, just as one man's action (Adam) had a devastating effect on mankind, another man's action (Jesus) also had an effect on mankind, one brought death and the other brought life, one brought sin and the other brought forgiveness.

It reminds me that it's a bit like the game connect 4: where you must get 4 of the same colour counters in a row…. The two counters are:

Adam=sin=death=damnation

Jesus=forgiveness=life=eternity

I know which counter I am playing with……Jesus: He has won the game, game over, He is the winner.

Breathe

Yesterday's message from Rev John Jackson was about breathing and it got me thinking.
 I looked on the internet and it said the following: Breathing is essential to keep us alive, because every living cell in the body needs a continual supply of oxygen. Inside each cell, oxygen combines with food molecules in a chemical reaction called oxidation, which releases energy. This energy powers every process in the human body. Not only does breathing provide your body with necessary oxygen, but it also rids the body of waste like carbon dioxide. To get rid of carbon dioxide, your blood delivers it to the capillaries surrounding your alveoli. In the alveoli, the carbon dioxide moves into the lungs, where it leaves the body when you exhale.

 So, as well as breathing in we need to breathe out, we breathe in the things of God and breathe out the things that are not. Most of us have no trouble in breathing but there are some people that for various reasons need help, they may need an inhaler to help with shortness of breath, a tracheotomy to aid breathing when there may be a blockage or a life support machine if a person is unable to breathe for themselves, this machine or these aids help people breathe. Or we may need the kiss of life to help us start breathing again.

When God breathed life into Adam it could be similar to the kiss of life, before Adam received breath, he was lifeless, that same life was also breathed into us as we are a by-product from Adam. Before we accepted God into our life, I suppose we could be said to be lifeless, yes, we were breathing, but breathing in things that could kill us.

I remember a time when I was laughing so much, I could hardly breathe and then there's been times when I've cried so hard I can't catch my breath. There are times, almost daily that I need a spiritual breathing aid, I need God to be my life support when I am unable to breathe for myself (if I'm in a trial for example). I need Him to be my tracheotomy when my breathing is blocked by things of the world; I need Him to be my inhaler when I fall short.

Open Wide

Yesterday I went to the dentist as I have been having tooth ache, I knew one of my teeth would need work on, however, when she examined my teeth she found further damage, I had to have an x ray and the tooth that was hurting was even worse that I had thought or could see, and the dentist also found another hole in one of my teeth. I was quite shocked as I had no other symptoms for my other teeth and so wasn't expecting bad news.

It kinda remind me that sometimes we can't always see clearly what is going on inside of us, or what damage we have, I suffer with mental health problems and was aware of one of the causes, but, when I was examined by a professional I was shocked at just how much other unseen damage I had, she more or less had to do an oral x-ray and it showed up things not visible to the eye.

Sometimes we may say something to another person and from the outside we seem to think it hasn't affected them, but, just like an x-ray if we were to look inside them and see the damage we had caused. Lately whenever someone asks me how I am, I reply 'I'm fine', I could have tears rolling down my face, but I will tell them I'm fine, I've learned over the past couple months that that's the best answer to give, whilst some may accept that,

God is my x-ray machine and can see deep inside, see the things that I can't even see.

Before the dentist could put in my filling, she had to first clean out my tooth, otherwise there may be trapped food in there that will get filled in and cause further pain. The dentist then told me how to look after my teeth and prescribed special toothpaste to help prevent further cavities.

Before God can fill my holes, my cavities, He needs to clean me up first, remove all the bad

food as such and prepare me, fill the hole and
then tell me how to look after myself so that I
don't create further holes, voids in my life.

When did you last have an x ray?

Spring clean

My son likes to think I'm a clean freak and takes great pleasure in telling me, I however, disagree. I've noticed when I've gone shopping and I'm looking for cleaning products I'm taken aback at the different ranges, you have sprays to clean kitchen, sprays to clean toilet, sprays to clean bath, sprays to clean shower, sprays to clean windows. They all claim to have some great cleansing power that can cut through grease or to leave your floor sparkling. The adverts on TV just reinforce this. Sometimes I don't know which product to buy.

At home my bath has a stain in it, I think it was from when I was having my hallway redecorated and they used the bath to wash out the paint brushes, however, no matter how many times I clean the bath the stain is still there, I use bleach, I leave the spray to soak, I scrub, I sweat but the stain is still there.

My son has a white shirt, and it had that many stains on it nothing was going to get rid of it so he had to throw the shirt away.

It got me thinking, I have stains in me which I call sin, and I've tried over the years to get rid of them, I smoked, I cried, I self-harmed, I ran away, I ignored it, but the sin was still there. Then one day I came across a cleanser that I hadn't seen before, it said it could remove all my sins/stains, dirt, that I didn't need to soak in it, scrub it, it was instant, I could be whiter than snow, I could lose all my guilty stains. Well, I had to buy this cleanser but when I went to find out the price, I couldn't find one, I was told it was free, the price had already been paid. Jesus had paid it all, He was and is the only one who can cleanse us and make us whole. He is a bit like ronseal, He does what He says he will do. I just needed to confess and ask for forgiveness. Simples!

Psalm 51:7 says purify me with hyssop, and I shall be clean; Wash me, and I shall be whiter than snow.

I'm hungry

I have a habit that when I am bored, I start eating, or when I'm hungry I just eat and eat-albeit mainly the wrong things, but I'm hungry and need to feed the hunger.

It got me thinking, we are all hungry for something. Some are hungry for love and will seek it from the wrong people or places. Some are lonely and will feed on friendships where they are just being abused. Some feed their addictions and habits i.e., gambling drugs. Some are hungry to be liked or accepted so will compromise their morals to be accepted. Some are hungry to look different, so they feed that hunger by having constant plastic surgery.

I know that when I am hungry and I snack on sweets or crisps it is not going to fill me up for very long, it will maybe take the initial hunger away for a short while, but ultimately, I will be hungry again.

Those hungers mentioned above will not sustain us. They are temporary fillings. We will keep being hungry for love, acceptance, friendship etc. The only way we can ever be filled fully is by bread, not the actual food bread, but the bread of life. In John 6:35 Jesus said I am the bread of life and he who comes to me shall never hunger. What are we feeding our hunger today? Will it sustain us?

Be blessed

A call to remember

Yesterday Rev John Jackson preached on the topic a call to remember, this was in line with it being remembrance Sunday, and it got me thinking, there is a saying that an elephant never forgets, or sometimes I have to put reminders in my phone so that I remember appointments and so forth, but there are some things that I remember that I shouldn't, and I remember them with a passion. I remember all the physical and emotional abuse, I remember the name calling, the fear of dread, I remember being scared to come home, I remember seeing my sister lying in the mortuary, I remember people rejecting me, I remember it all too well. I seem to struggle to remember good things like having a laugh with my friends, the antics my son would get up to when he was younger, I forget to remember the love people have and still show me, I forget to remember where God has brought me from. When I look in the mirror, I remember the hurtful comments but fail to remember that I am fearfully and wonderfully made. I forget to remember that God loves me, that He is a very present help in time of trouble. I forget to remember that no weapon formed against me shall prosper, I forget to remember that greater is He that is in me than he that is in the world. I forget to remember that I am blessed and highly favoured. I forget to remember who God says I am.

In **Isaiah 43:18 it says "Forget the former things; do not dwell on the past.** Dwelling on the past stops me from living in the present and denies me from living in the future, I think history will repeat itself. Dwelling on the past won't change it, it won't erase it, it just makes it fresh, I give life to it, it's like I am resuscitating it when it has already died. If I remember all the times, I have been rejected then it makes it hard to form relationships as I will think they will reject me too. It's very hard if I'm honest when negative things outweigh the positive things to remember. I try and I fail but I have to keep trying and to remember God has a purpose for me.

Can you hold me now?

Pastor John Jackson said something to me on Monday that God holds you when you don't have the strength to hold Him and I was like Pastor you don't understand what I'm saying, but it got me thinking, when a baby is born and for the first maybe 4 months it doesn't have the strength to hold up their head, they cannot support themselves by standing, they need someone to hold them, to lift them up, to be their strength. When my son was a baby, he never had the strength to hold his bottle, I had to be his strength otherwise he would not be able to eat. Gradually that baby develops strength and can rely less on their parent. The baby doesn't know it's been supported, sometimes God holds us, and we don't even know, we may think we are relying on our own strength when in fact it is Gods strength that is made perfect in our weakness. This scripture says that it is ok to be weak at times because that is when the power of Christ can work in/through me **2 Corinthians 12:9**. The following lyrics sums it all up really 'You **are my strength, strength like no other, strength like no other reaches to me, in the fullness of your grace, in the power of your name, you lift me up, you lift me up'.**

It then got me thinking further, I was looking at **John 7:37 where Jesus cried if any man is thirsty, let him come to me and drink.** To be thirsty is due to lack of water, nakedness is a lack of clothes, hunger is a lack of food, being broke or poor is a lack of money, being cold is a lack of heat. Drought is lack of rain/water, not trusting God is a lack of faith. We all at times lack something i.e., love, friends, food, money etc. but just like that scripture, Jesus is saying come unto me, I can and will supply your needs according to my riches in glory.

Psalm 34:10 says' but those who seek the lord lack no good thing' and James 1:4 says 'and let steadfastness have its full effect, that you may be perfect and complete, lacking in nothing

Mental health 1

The problem with my mental health is that sometimes I find it extremely hard to cope with my emotions, imagine you have a tap that can't turn off properly, so it drips constantly all day and all night, you try to drown out the sound or ignore it, but you know it's there. Or imagine you can hear a cricket in the grass, you can't see it to move it, but it's there making a constant noise. Not going to lie this past week has been challenging, my mind hasn't switched off, I've felt threatened, I've felt scared, my mind was working more than overtime, it was plotting to kill me, that would have been the best outcome. I couldn't even say to my mind PEACE BE STILL! I couldn't talk to no-one, and no one actually truly understood. How can you explain to someone else when you can barely explain it to yourself? An animal or a baby for example cannot tell you verbally when they are in pain or where the pain is, they make suggestions i.e., cry or whimper, they may refuse food, they may not use that particular limb. They know they are in pain: they want you to know they are in pain, but the communication is blocking the transmission. I couldn't communicate to anyone the sheer deep distress I was in. suicide seemed the only option.

Last night I felt I was drowning, I was being drowned emotionally, I couldn't find or see the lifeguard, I was like Jesus where are you, throw me the life jacket. My emotions imprisoned me; I'd be given a life sentence without parole. I was dying. I cried so much I grazed my eye. Mental health comes in all shapes and sizes and guises, I can look you dead in the face and say I'm ok, I'll even smile when deep down I'm plotting how I can hurt myself. Mental health is nothing to be ashamed off and you shouldn't feel guilty for being affected.

I share this not to expose myself, but to let another person who maybe feeling the same that they are not alone, I feel alone because mental health is real, it is real for Christians, it is real for me. Peeps I truly need your prayers, my fight has gone, my energy has gone. I don't want my hope to be gone

Give it to Him

On Monday my son asked me to take his driving licence to work so a friend can verify his identity. Thursday afternoon he asked me if I had taken it. I replied no, he wasn't impressed so I replied you never gave me the licence. I knew he needed it done but he needed to give me the licence.

This got me thinking, sometimes I say to God, God why haven't you taken this pain away or why have you not done this or why have I not been forgiven for this, and God is simply saying to me Michelle, you never gave it to me. How can I expect God to heal my pain if I don't give it to Him, or, how can I be forgiven if I don't give my sins to Him? God knows my pain He knows my sins, but He is waiting for me to give them over to Him.

When I give it God, I need to make sure I give it to Him totally, not withholding anything, not looking to do an exchange or refund later.

1 Peter 5:7 says **casting all your anxieties on him, because he cares for you.** The song line that says 'oh what peace we often forfeit, oh what needless pain we bear, all because we do not carry everything to God in prayer' reminds me that if I don't carry/give EVERYTHING to God in prayer I carry needless pain. Sometimes when I have a headache and I don't take a tablet for it, I carry needless pain in my head, the solution is there but I refuse to use it.

Be blessed today as you take everything to God in prayer

Get a grip

I was at church yesterday and there was a baby being held by someone and as I looked, I could see the baby grip onto the person holding them. They didn't want to fall and although the baby was young, they sensed pending danger. The baby needed to feel secure that come what may they will not let you go. Or sometimes when a toddler grabs something they shouldn't and you're trying to take it off them, that they grip it so tight with all their strength as they are not giving it up. Or imagine you are a bodybuilder in a competition, and you are lifting some heavy weights, you grip on to the bar so tight, although your knees maybe bending and shaking, you know you cannot afford to let it go as you may lose or even injure yourself.

It got me thinking, when God holds us, He grips us so tight, He is not letting us go and nothing can prise His grip, likewise when we hold on to God we need to grip Him like our life depends on it. That come what may we aren't letting go.

Siamese twins, Lego bricks, parents and children, egg whites and yolks and certain liquids for example are things that can be separated. However, not everything that is joined together is to be separated. When we are joined with God then death, nor life, nor angels, nor principalities, nor powers, nor things present or to come, nor height or depth, nor any other creature cannot and should not separate a believer from the Love of God (Romans 8:38-39)

Be blessed today as you grip on to God

Be healed

I have a cut on my arm, don't know how it happened, it started to heal and scab over, now, I have a habit of picking my scabs so of course I had to pick it, it hurt a little and then started to bleed but at least the scab was gone, because I picked the scab off the cut needed to start the healing process again, another scab would form and I would pick it off, even when it hurt I'm still continuing and the cut would need healing again. This cycle continued until well, it's continuing, the scab is not so big now, but it's now left a scar that may not fade away. Even when the scab is not bothering me, I know it's there and it needs to be picked. I can't leave it alone to let the healing process do its job. If I keep picking the scab it takes longer to heal.

This got me thinking, sometimes God is trying to heal my past, He will bring people into my life, provide sources of help but the minute the healing process begins I pick the scab and let the hurt back into my life, God will then close the door on the past again and once again I pick the scab and let the hurt back into my life, at the same time I'm praying to God for healing? How will my cut heal if I don't leave it alone, how can my past stay in the past if I keep bringing into the present. How can I make sure I'm not left with a big scar emotionally? God is saying Michelle leave the scab alone, it's there for a purpose, a scab protects the cut from more injury and infection and give the skin cells underneath a chance to heal, you can't see what's going on under the scab, but we do know the healing process has started, the cut is being repaired

But I will restore you to health and heal your wounds,' declares the LORD" ~ Jeremiah 30:17 LORD my God, I called to you for help, and you healed me." ~ Psalm 30:2

Be blessed today

Black ice

Thursday was the first day I had driven my car since the weather on Sunday. I was a bit nervous as there was still some ice around, I drove at a steady pace and kept a good distance and when I had to brake I did it slowly. The thing that scared me the most was the black ice. It is called "black ice" as it is often camouflaged and looks the same as the road's surface, making it hard to spot before you walk or drive on it. The ice itself is not black and as it is almost invisible to drivers there is a risk of skidding and for pedestrians a risk of slipping.

This got me thinking, sometimes in life things may look as if they are going ok and then suddenly a 'black ice' situation appears and for some people and I will use myself as an example I spin out of control. With black ice if your back wheels turn in one direction you need to turn the wheel in that direction too as to avoid your car spinning off the road. I remember one black ice situation and because I turned a different way than what I should have I spun out of control, skidded and crashed emotionally and spiritually. I hadn't seen the danger as it was camouflaged.

I needed to have approached that situation differently. Just like driving in black ice I needed to stay calm, reduce my speed, not brake suddenly, not panic, maintain my speed. What I need to remember is that God is in control, He is in control in the black ice, in the rain, in the sun, whatever the condition or situation He's still in control

Be blessed today as we remember God is in control

Light it up

Yesterday at our Christmas carol service pastor gave a demonstration, the lights were switched off and he asked us to close our eyes tightly, we kept them closed for a couple minutes and then he switched the lights on, our eyes remained closed, but we could still see the light somehow. This is how it is with God, no matter how dark our situation, when God shows up, the darkness must go, once the light of the world shines into the darkness of our desperation it is no longer dark, for once a flicker of light appears, the room for example is no longer dark. During the candlelight service we each held a battery operated tea light and as the lights were switched off we sang the song **'light of the world, you stepped down into darkness'** and it's a song I've sung many times before but this time, as I looked at the tea light, it was as if I was looking at God shining in the dark, it may not have been a bright light or a big light, but it was light, the room that was once dark was no longer.

After hearing of the sad news earlier that morning of the fatal car crash darkness fell on me, I felt so down, it really affected me, but, as I looked at the tea light, I felt encouraged, darkness only lasts for a while and then the SUN has to rise, darkness in my life only lasts for a while and then the SON has to rise.

Be blessed today as we remember **John 8:12....**
Jesus says, "I AM the light of the world, whoever follows me will not walk in darkness, but will have the light of life."

It's not a race

Growing up I used to love running, I thought I was pretty good at it and aspired of being an athlete. My favourite was the 100m or the 400m relay. It involved speed so you could be the winner. If a race didn't involve speed, I wasn't interested, it was all about getting to the finishing line first.

On the other hand, marathons are long distance running races, mainly 26 miles. Because of the distance constant speed is not likely going to help you win, you need to pace yourself, you may start of fast, slow down halfway through, you may even walk for some of it. I've seen some instances where someone for example has taken all day to do a complete a marathon, speed wasn't necessarily a factor for that person but to finish the marathon. Sometimes I've seen others help someone they see struggling, they may become a crutch for them or be someone to lean on, these people learned that it's also important to help someone else cross the finish line. Sometimes you can see the pain on someone's face as they struggle to continue, they know quitting is not an option so even if it takes them all week, on bended knees, they are crossing that finishing line.

It got me thinking, the Christian journey is not a 100m dash or sprint, in **Ecclesiastes 9:11 says the race is not given to the swift nor the strong but unto them that endure to the end."**

I looked at the word swift and it means happening quickly or promptly, and being strong doesn't necessarily mean you're a winner, I've watched programmes like the strongest man in the world and there are still losers. So being strong and being swift does not guarantee you will finish the Christian race. It's all about endurance, in all weathers, conditions, trials, pain, heartaches, troubles, if on bended knees, as long as we endure to the end, we will cross that line.

Endure means to hold out against, to bear, to suffer, abide. The song goes 'nobody told me the road would be easy' but if we only hold on even by broken fingernails, we will make it!!

Be blessed as you endure to the end

Fix me

Yesterday to my horror I realised my MOT was due to expire, I panicked, the usual place I go to wasn't answering their phone and I didn't know where else to go, thankfully I found a garage round the corner and decided to put my trust in them. I left my car with them and came home, a couple of hours later they rang and said my car had FAILED. I was gutted, he explained it was going to be a big job, thankfully it wasn't the case in the end, but it got me thinking, the MOT is an annual **test of vehicle safety, roadworthiness aspects and exhaust emissions required** in the United Kingdom for most vehicles over three years old. So, yesterday when my car eventually passed the MOT after having the repair done it became roadworthy again, but, next week it may not be roadworthy, something may happen to the vehicle without me knowing that only an annual inspection could detect. The car may drive the same but for example to emissions could be wrong. Sometimes it feels like at new year's eve

I do an MOT test, I see if I am are safe, worthy and what we emit out of my mouth is correct, generally I fail the MOT but then I try and repair what was wrong, it may last for a while but eventually something goes wrong and I need to go to the mechanic (Jesus) and ask for an internal inspection and fix what is wrong/fix what the eye cannot see.

The song 'Fix Me' comes to mind and it simply says **Fix me Jesus, fix me / Oh fix me, oh fix me, oh fix me / Fix me Jesus, fix me / Fix me for my home on high / Fix me Jesus, fix me / Fix me for the by and by / Fix me Jesus, fix me.**

Be blessed today

Stay afloat

I've never really enjoyed swimming and I used to hate it when we had to do it at secondary school. I remember once when we were aiming for our swimming badges and I had to swim a length, I FROZE! The thought of having to jump in at the deep end scared me, I was going to drown, there is no way I can make it back up again. Having many words of comfort and encouragement and with the help of a pole I jumped in.

This got me thinking, the fear of drowning was real for me, I perceived a threat and responded.

I looked on the internet for information about drowning and came across this.

SIGNS THAT MAY INDICATE A PERSON IS DROWNING
The victim is rarely able to call for help, an active drowning victim will bob in and out of the water with his or her mouth being just above

the surface of the water. The person is not making forward progress either.

Drowning persons are often desperate and would grab at the closest thing to them with a grip of death. It is a harrowing experience to watch someone drown without any hope of help; or trying to help and getting drowned in the process.
Float don't swim to avoid drowning.

There are times as a child of God that I have felt that I am drowning, that I'm going under and can't get up, that I can't call out for help, that I'm not making any forward progress. It's a horrible feeling. I don't want to drown but I haven't got the strength to stay afloat. I feel the waves of sin drowning me, the waves of not being good enough drowning me, the waves of heaviness taking me under. The waves of pain and hurt and shame washing over me. Sometimes you may not know a person is drowning, often in films we see people waving their arms to indicate they are drowning but the other person thinks they are waving hello and waves back. Sometimes we may shout out 'help, I'm drowning' but because the other person doesn't know what to do in an emergency the person drowns. There are also times when a person is trying to rescue another person from drowning and the drowning person drowns the other person because they panic and thrash about for example.

There is also what's known as dry drowning, secondary drowning where the symptoms appear maybe 24 hours later

Isaiah 43:2 says When you go through deep waters, I will be with you. When you go through rivers of difficulty, you will not drown. When you walk through the fire of oppression, you will not be burned up; the flames will not consume you.

Be blessed today as we become lifeguards for one another. We should not be drowning!

One more push

When I was in labour with my son and at the stage of having to 'push' I found myself exhausted, having been in labour for the last 26 hours, I barely had any energy left to push. However, if I didn't push then my son could not be born, the 'push' stage was the final part of my labour, I had endured the labour pains but now it was time for it to be over.

I remember pushing a couple of times and then I was knackered, the midwife kept saying, we're nearly there, just a few more pushes. To be honest it was more than pushes, it was bearing down, teeth grimaced and giving everything, you have just to push the child down. When the midwife was saying keep pushing, I wasn't sure if she actually understood the pain I was going through, the strength that I no longer had to push, the giving up feeling. I just couldn't do it.

However, as mentioned earlier, to give up pushing would mean there would be no outcome. My son could possibly be born by caesarean but that may cause further problems. Regardless of how tired I was, how weak I felt, I had no other option but to push. I had to push for the pain to end, I had to push to see the outcome. I had to push. The midwife couldn't push for me, a birthing partner couldn't push for me, they could encourage me, but I had to be the one to push. I had to push until the baby was born, until something happened, I wasn't pushing for the fun of it. Something was needed to be birthed

It's a bit like that spiritually, sometimes when I'm in pain, or going through a trial or feeling low or whatever it may be, I just want to give up, I have no energy to carry on and I may tell my pastor how I'm feeling, and he will reply and say push. I'm like do you do not see that I am weak, in pain, but, like labour, I need to push my way through this season. I need to PUSH…. pray until something happens, praise until something happens, perceiver until something happens, press until something happens.

Something must happen, when you push a door it opens, when you push a pram it moves, when you push someone, they fall over, something happens.

Philippians 4:13 says I can do all things through Christ who gives me strength...... strength to push, strength to hold, strength like no other reaches to me, Christ is our strength and in Him we can push.

Be blessed today

On fleek

I like to have my eyebrows done but when I do, I always look at the eyebrows of the person doing it. If their eyebrows don't look good or on fleek as they say, then I'm a bit apprehensive to use them as I feel if their eyebrows aren't on fleek then they won't be able to do mine. It could be the fact that yes, they can do eyebrows quite good, but my decision is based on an outward appearance. The same I suppose goes for when I go dentist, if their teeth aren't shining white how can you give me advice on my teeth, or if I go hairdressers and their hair is not presented nice, I have little confidence in them being able to do my hair. It could be that the hairdresser is working 6 days a week all hours of the day so may not have as much time as they want to spend on their hair.

It got me thinking, likewise there may be some people who want to go to church or give there life to the Lord but they may for example be looking at me, looking at how I act, what I say etc and if I am not behaving as I should they may decide nah it's not for me. they may think if Michelle buckles at the first hurdle, then what's the point, what hope do I have. I suppose what I'm saying is that people tend to look on the outside appearance and at what we say and do etc.

I need to remind myself that someone somewhere is watching me, maybe on the verge of making that decision and I don't want to be the reason they say nah God is not for them.

The lyrics to a song by Junior Tucker remind me that **"The only Jesus that people see Is the Jesus in you and me Let your light so shine, I want the world to see just how much You love me, show them Your grace and Your mercy, use me to advertise, so they will realize You're the only God who sets the captives free"**

Be blessed today as we remember we are an advertisement for the King of Kings

It shall pass

I've never had a kidney stone that I know off as usually they go undetected and be passed out painlessly in the urine, and I hope I never get one.
but there are times when the kidney stone blocks part of the urinary system and I know of someone who this happened to, and I know it was PAINFUL (the kidney stone was scratching the kidney or ureter)
According to the net after the kidney stone has formed our body will naturally try to pass it out when we go to the toilet.

Kidney stones are generally small so I was thinking how can something so small cause so much pain, It got me thinking, sometimes in life we go through trials and for some of us it may be small like the kidney stone but cause the most amount of pain, as we pass through that trial/situation/storm the pain we feel is indescribable, but we have to pass through it, there is no other way, it cannot remain with us.

To pass through means we come out the other side/end. The kidney stone must come out, it may require an operation if it is bigger than normal, or it may require being broken down by lasers. Sometimes we may need prayer or intercession from others to help break down the storm into manageable sizes that although still painful, it will pass. It may take a while for the stone to pass through.

There's a song by a group called Rizen and it goes a little like this "**the Lord is right by your side, He's able to provide, whatever you need, just believe and it will come to pass.**

Whatever we are facing right now, be rest assured that it will pass, it may be painful, it may be hard, it may take time, but it will come to pass.

Be blessed today

Clean break

I remember when I was around 14 for some random reason, I wanted to break my arm, I wanted a cast, I don't know why, I just did and I remember telling someone to twist my arm and then hit it with a rounder's bat, anyway, it didn't work, and my arm has remained unbroken ever since.

There are some people who have the misfortune of breaking their bone in such a way that it has be to be set in the right way, if it is not the bone still may heal but it won't be fully healed. The limb affected may cause mobility problems or may not be able to be used again. If the bone is not healed properly the doctors may need to break the bone again in order to re-set it.

It got me thinking, when we come to God broken, He fixes us, He heals us, He makes us whole, He knows how to heal our brokenness without it causing further problems, it is not a temporary healing.

We may be broken in spirit, body, mind, I know there's times when it feels like my heart and spirit has been broken but God said in **Psalm 51: 17 the sacrifices of God are a broken spirit, a broken and contrite heart God will not despise.** God wants to fix us, a surgeons job is not to see a broken limb and leave it, he has to fix it, God does not desire for us to remain broken, He is waiting to fix us, but we have to come to Him to be fixed, if my car is broken down, I have to either call a mechanic or take it to a garage, it won't get fixed by itself and I have to tell the mechanic its broken, could maybe give some indication of what's wrong.

The lyrics to kirk Franklins song goes **"come ye broken hearted, come ye weary soul, there is healing water that can make you whole, and it flows from the veins of Jesus my Saviour, my healer, redeemer a lover so true, your healing is here, forgiveness is here, salvation is here,**

acceptance is here, deliverance is here, love is here that can make you whole"

Be blessed today, you don't have to remain broken.

Waste

I'm not really an expert on the human body but I know that mainly daily we need to remove waste from our body, this is what is called excretion.

Excretion is an essential process in which waste products are removed from the body. Without excretion, waste products build up in the body and cause serious health issues. The excretory system is important for many reasons. Similarly, to your need to take out the garbage, to prevent nasty smells, clutter, and invasions by other organisms, the excretory is like taking out our garbage. Problems can develop from malfunctions of the excretory system. (Taken from the internet).

If we don't remove our waste it clogs up, may cause us stomach or back pains, it was never designed to remain in us, sometimes we may need to take supplements to help us remove the waste.

It got me thinking, just like how we need to remove waste daily, we also need to remove our sins from us daily, if we don't remove our sins then they too can clog us up, make us ill, give us clutter and make us feel dirty. There are some sin's that we may not know we have or even see it as a sin, which is why I ask God to forgive things that I may not class as sins.

Sometimes people may think they have no sin, they may I've not murdered anyone or lied, but it says in **Romans 3:23 For all have sinned, and come short of the glory of God and 1 John 1:8 it says If we claim to be without sin, we deceive ourselves and the truth is not in us. Psalm 51:5 states Behold, I was brought forth in iniquity, and in sin my mother conceived me.**

Be blessed today as we ask for forgiveness

Unchangeable

Over time technology has advanced, gone are the days when we had to get up to adjust the volume or change the channel on the television, encyclopaedias have now been replaced by google, maps are a thing of the past thanks to sat navs, mobile phones have that many functions now than the standard brick Motorola of the 90's. TV's are smart, we've gone from vinyl to tape to cd to now streaming, Betamax and vhs have now been replaced by blu ray and Netflix, I don't even have to get out of my seat if I want to turn my light off as my Alexa echo plus will do that for me. I suppose change is important in some aspects, as time goes by our needs change, some of the changes are good and some aren't , I remember years ago if it was someone's birthday I would buy them a card, now I just send them a quick message on my phone sometimes abbreviated the word happy birthday to hbd, I no longer have to get out of my car to tell someone I am outside their house,

I just call them from my phone. Inevitably things will change further as time goes by.

However, during change we can be assured that God will never change, His word will never change, His love for us will never change, His plans for our lives won't change, His plans to see us prosper won't change, His desire to bless us won't change, HE WON'T CHANGE.

In **Hebrews 13:8 it says Jesus Christ is the same yesterday, today and forever** and Smokie Norful lyrics says **"I am the Lord I changeth not, and I won't forget, nor have I forgot, and everything works according to My plan, I am God, trust me, I got the whole world in My hands"**

Be blessed today

Don't stay down

Something my pastor said to me yesterday got me thinking, when a baby is learning to walk part of the process is that they fall down, however when they fall down, they get back up and try again, they don't just quit at the first setback. An athlete for example doing the hurdles may trip over one or even more and fall but they get back up and finish the race. When you ride a bike and fall off you get back up and try again. If you ice skate and fall you get back up. If you slip in the ice, you get back up, you don't stay on the ground

When we fall as Christians and we will fall we have to get back up it may be a big fall, may be a small fall. May be a hard fall that leaves us feeling bruised, battered and broken, but we must get back up. God didn't design us to stay down. May take time getting back up, may need a little help getting back up. Sometimes it's a lot easier said than done and I speak from experience, but I'm here, I got back up, not sure how some of the time.

The song that comes to mind is by Donnie McClurkin called Fall Down and it goes **"We fall down, but we get up, a saint is just a sinner who fell down, but we couldn't stay there, and got up"**

Proverbs 24:16 says for though a righteous man falls seven times, he will rise again, but the wicked stumble into calamity and Jeremiah 8:4 "Say to them, 'This is what the LORD says: "'When people fall down, do they not get up? When someone turns away, do they not return?

Be blessed today as you get back up

Kill that root

As an experienced gardener (not really) when you plant a seed, you don't just plant it and leave it, you have to water it or give it plant food to help it grow. It can't grow unless it has been fed. The seed won't develop, and it will die.

It got me thinking, when we plant a seed such as doubt, for that seed to grow and develop we need to water/feed it, the seed then grows until it is formed.

An example of the above could be us feeding doubt by giving it our attention, time and validation, and once fed the seed of doubt grows and can blossom into a negative mind set with fear being its roots. Lust for example according to **James 1:15 grows 'after desire has been conceived, it gives birth to sin; and sin, when it is full-grown, gives birth to death'**

I'm having to learn not to water my fear, doubt, hate, anger, malice and etc etc so that it will die, it's hard because sometimes I don't even know I'm feeding it.

However, there are some plants like the Japanese knotweed which grows at an alarming rate and is very difficult to control or even kill. It has an invasive root system and strong growth. To eradicate the plant the roots, need to be killed. Likewise, some sins can be like that. We need weed killer to destroy the roots. We don't want the sin to become full grown so that it leads to death. We need the master sin killer Jesus to destroy the root.

So how do we do this? well according to **2 Corinthians 10:5 by casting down imaginations, and every high thing that exalteth itself against the knowledge of God and bringing into captivity every thought to the obedience of Christ.**

Sometimes when I worry, I imagine all kind of scenarios, scenarios that haven't even happened and probably won't happen, to me that is an example of casting down imaginations.

Be blessed today

Exchange rate

I was watching a cooking channel yesterday and it was filmed in Vietnam, the presenter was going round trying different foods, he had a plateful of different stuff and asked how much it was, the reply was 25,000 Vietnamese dong, this sounded quite a lot until he said that works out a roughly $1.

In the above scenario us changing US dollars or even pounds into Vietnamese dong, you get more for your money, say you exchanged £100 and got 680,000 dong, that money could go a long way and last a lot longer whereas if you exchanged £100 for American dollars you may only get $80 (random guess).

It got me thinking, we have all received something far greater than what we have paid in, when Jesus said in John 19:30 "IT IS FINISHED" a great exchange took place, Jesus exchanged His sinless state and took on our sin, He exchanged our unrighteousness for His righteousness, He exchanged death for life, He exchanged our shame for His glory, He exchanged us being rejected from God to being reconciled with Him. It cost God everything and it cost us nothing, it cost Jesus being shamed, beaten, mocked, humiliated, He was scourged and by that I mean He was beaten with an implement designed to cause severe bodily punishment, according to the internet it was a handle which several cords or leather thongs were attached with pieces of jagged bone or metal to make the blow more painful and effective.

He took my place on the cross, an exchange rate I can never repay, He saw that my worth was worth it all.

In the words of the song **"I'll never know how much it cost to see my sins upon the cross, so here I am to worship, here I am to bow down, here I am to say that you're my king, you're altogether lovely, altogether worthy, altogether wonderful to me"**.

Be blessed today in this lent season. Jesus exchanged His life for YOU.

Greater in store

I have a technic hi fi but unfortunately it can't play usb or micro sd nor does it have DAB radio, so I was on the lookout for a new system. My son had borrowed his friend's micro hi fi for his birthday and it had all the specs I was after, I plugged it in, turned the volume up halfway and thought yes this is great, so went ahead and ordered it. About an hour after I had paid for it my son said mom, it's not that good, I tried the system again with the volume on its highest and it sounded muffled. That had to get refunded. I then brought an amazon echo because again I was under the impression it could do all I needed it to do as I could play my Spotify music and would also take up less space. I then went ahead and brought one, spent 2 hours trying to link it to my Bluetooth, wouldn't connect so I rang amazon for help, I gave them the serial number and was shocked to hear that the device was reported as lost/stolen. That had to get refunded too.

I was a bit disillusioned by now, I just wanted a new hi fi system. Anyway, on the Monday I went into a town and popped into a shop and what did I behold………. A Sony Bluetooth speaker with the wattage I was after and all the other functions I needed. I was on cloud nine, I paid for it and took it home and I am so pleased with it. It got me thinking, the problem with the first 2 hi-fis were there because there was something greater in store for me, for the same price. God can be like that, sometimes things don't work out as we had hoped, didn't get that promotion, didn't get the marriage, didn't get the car, not because God doesn't want us to have good things, but, because He has so much greater things in store than that promotion-maybe not getting the promotion prompts you to look for a new job with better money or working conditions, that partner you thought was your future spouse may not be as God has someone greater in mind for you

James 1:17 Every good thing given, and every perfect gift is from above, coming down from

the Father of lights, with whom there is no variation or shifting shadow.

Be blessed today

Falseness

The thing about having dentures is that they may look good but can sometimes be useless, they aren't as strong as real teeth, may have trouble eating certain foods, aren't permanent, may irritate your gum and probably need some glue to keep them in place. They are removable false teeth in effect. Dentures do not function like normal teeth, it takes time to learn how to use them properly, food needs to be cut up smaller and placed on back teeth to balance chewing.

It got me thinking, in life we may come across false things, i.e., people, friends, prophets, teachers

The following scriptures talk about False teachers, evidently, they are no good for you, just like the dentures, they may look good but be of no use, no strong or firm foundation that you can hold onto

Ezekiel 13:9 My hand will be against the prophets who see false visions and utter lying divinations. They will not belong to the council of my people or be listed in the records of Israel, nor will they enter the land of Israel. Then you will know that I am the Sovereign LORD.

Jeremiah 23.16 This is what the LORD Almighty says: "Do not listen to what the prophets are prophesying to you; they fill you with false hopes. They speak visions from their own minds,
not from the mouth of the LORD

Matthew 24:24 For false messiahs and false prophets will appear and perform great signs and wonders to deceive, if possible, even the elect.

Galatians 1:7-8 which is really no gospel at all. Evidently some people are throwing you into confusion and are trying to pervert the gospel of Christ.,

As well as false teachers and prophets there are those who bring false doctrine

2 John 1:10-11 If there come any unto you, and bring not this doctrine, receive him not into your house, neither bid him God speed: For he that biddeth him God speed is partaker of his evil deeds.

Romans 16:17-18 I urge you, brothers and sisters, to watch out for those who cause divisions and put obstacles in your way that are contrary to the teaching you have learned. Keep away from them.

Be blessed today as you study God's word for yourself so that you can be aware of false teachings and doctrines

We fall down

I remember a few years ago when the weather was bad and there was ice on the ground, I was walking back from town with my son and when this man fell because of the ice, immediately people were running to him to see if he was ok and if he needed any help, it's usually our instinct to do this.

In the above scenario we may help that person get back up, they may not be strong enough by themselves, they may refuse our offer of help as they feel they can get back up by themselves or they may want our help, but pride gets in their way.

It got me thinking, as Christians we should be doing the same, if our brother or sister in Christ falls in the faith we should be going to them and ask if they need any help getting back up, again, they may refuse our help, may not need our help or pride becomes an issue, there are also times that even though we may need help we have to pick ourselves back up with no help, but, in my opinion the offer of help should always be there. We will all fall at some time or another, may be a mighty fall, may be a tiny fall, but we are our brother/sisters' keepers.

Ecclesiastes 4:9-12 Two people are better than one because together they have a good reward for their hard work. If one falls, the other can help his friend get up. But how tragic it is for the one who is all alone when he falls.

Psalm 145:14-16 The LORD helps the fallen and lifts those bent beneath their loads

Jeremiah 8:4 "Say to them, 'This is what the LORD says: "'When people fall down, do they not get up? When someone turns away, do they not return

Be blessed today as we help one another

Under the rock

I've always been a bit squeamish when it comes to bugs and worms for example, as a child I never really experimented much in the garden, picking up rocks to see what was underneath them or cutting a worm in two to see if it would still survive.

Sometimes when I would pick up a rock, I would see ants quickly scurrying away or a spider scuttle across the floor. Many animals like Lizards, Frogs, sometimes Fish, various forms of insects ranging from worms, spiders, crickets, to grubs. Snakes, bugs, beetles, ants also live among and under rocks.

The above animals most likely hide under the rock to regulate their body temperature and most importantly for their safety!! Safety from being another animals' dinner, safety from being trampled on from a human foot! What I also thought is that the rock they are hiding under needs to be big enough to hide them. I have this image of someone hiding behind a curtain and you can see their leg sticking out.

It got me thinking, the chorus that goes ' I am under the rock and the rock is higher than I, Jehovah hide, I am under the rock, go tell my enemies I am under the rock, Jehovah hide me, I am under the rock'. This chorus reminds me that even though I may not feel it I am under the rock, Jehovah is bigger, larger than anything and can hide me, hide me from the enemy, hide me from harm, from danger, Jehovah is higher than I am, we need to be asking always to lead me to the rock that is higher than I. only God can protect and keep us. Imagine the world's strongest man contest and they have to lift a 200-tonne boulder, they struggle, they sweat, they get frustrated, they may move it but not for a long time, the weight is unbearable. Jesus is a firm foundation; He is our ROCK and not even the strongest man can lift or move it!

We can find safety when we hide under the rock, if we remove ourselves from under the rock, we are prone to danger, the protection has gone.

Be blessed today

Emergency

I've noticed when driving that sometimes I'm not aware of the ambulance trying to get past me. The reason for this is that some ambulances when attending an emergency don't always use their blue siren sound to alert people. The lights are flashing but no sound so the ambulance at times has caught me unaware. I'm not sure why some have their sirens sounding and some don't. The internet said it is to do with the person's preference. Whatever the reason one thing we can be sure sound or not, as long as the lights are flashing it's an emergency.
It got me thinking, sometimes we as people are like the ambulance. We may be in an emergency situation and by our presence for example we may be crying, we may text or call someone, we let our sirens sound in whatever way we can to alert someone of our emergency. Then you may get some people who likewise are in an emergency situation but don't alert no one. You may only know of their emergency from observation, you may notice they are more

withdrawn, avoid contact with people, may look sad in their appearance and so forth. Both people are in an emergency, but you may notice one quicker than the other.

God sees us and knows us, He knows our situation, He knows the urgency and whether we have sirens sounding or not God attends to us. He knows before the situation appears and is already preparing to send His angels to dispatch to us. Just like when you call 911, 999 or 101 and they ask what the emergency or what service it is that you need, when we call on God He knows. He is our call handler and call dispatcher. He is our rescue.

I speak to myself as i write this. Keep me in your prayers pls

Be blessed today

Pain relief

When I was in labour, I had a few options of pain relief. I could have been a hero and decided to have no pain relief, but I didn't. Some of the options that are available are nitrous oxide also known as gas and air, pethidine and epidural and a TENS machine.

However, gas and air won't remove all the pain, but it can help reduce it and make it more bearable, it's easy to use and the women has control over it.

Pethidine is an injection placed into your thigh or bottom. I had mine in my thigh, it takes about 20 minutes to work and lasts for around 2-4 hours. I noticed that even after I had delivered my son, I still felt pain in my thigh for a while after.

An epidural is a local anaesthetic. It numbs the nerves that carry the pain to your brain. Most people find this takes away the pain completely and is mainly used for those in a long or painful labour. Only an anaesthetist can give the epidural. The problem with having an epidural is that you no longer know when you are having a contraction and it affects your mobility for a few hours. The TENS machine works by stimulating your body to release endorphins.

This got me thinking, we all go through some sort of pain throughout our lives', toothache, headache, cancer, etc. and when the pain gets to an unbearable state, we seek something to help lessen/remove the pain.

Whatever option we chose the pain is still their but how we deal with it or what medication we use is different for each person, some people have a high pain threshold, others not so.

Pain can be emotional or physical but they both require us to come to God. Some pain is essential as it shows our body is healing, if we break our arm for example, while it is healing, we may experience pain, or if someone has died and we are grieving, we know that the pain we feel is going towards our healing process. I've heard it be said that there is a purpose in our pain.

Be blessed today as we reflect on scriptures such as **Romans 8:18 'for I reckon** that the sufferings of this present time are not worthy to be compared with the glory which shall be revealed in us' and 2 Corinthians 1:5-6 'for as the sufferings of Christ abound in us, so our consolation also aboundeth in Christ, and whether we be afflicted, it is for your consolation and salvation, which is effectual in the enduring of the same sufferings which we also suffer; or whether we be comforted, it is for your consolation and suffering.'

Defender

Growing up I had the idea of becoming a barrister/lawyer, I wanted to defend people, I don't know why, I just felt a passion for it. Needless to say, I didn't pursue that career. I was watching a programme called Law and Order last week which is based mainly inside a court.

In a trial there are usually two side, the prosecution side, and the defense side. According to the internet the prosecution is the legal party responsible for presenting the case in a criminal trial against an individual accused of breaking the law and a criminal defense lawyer is a lawyer (mostly barristers) specializing in the defense of individuals and companies charged with criminal activity.

My thoughts are that the prosecutors job is to convince the jury that the accused is guilty, they will seek to find evidence to support their thought, they throw all sorts at them, dig up things from their past and make them out to be the worst person in the world and needs to convince the jury the person is guilty of the crime.

The defense's job is to convince the jury that the prosecutor's evidence is wrong, to provide a good character reference, that yes, they may have done some horrible things in the past but that is not who they are now, or, circumstances of their life may have caused them to commit a crime, they will try to show the jury that there are other possible explanations.

It got me thinking, the devil is the prosecutor in my own trial, trying to convince me that I am guilty of horrendous sins, he will find all sorts of evidence to back this up, if I told a lie 15 years ago, he will dig this up, if I gossiped last week, he will dig this up, if I didn't pray, pay my tithes and so forth, you name it, he will dig up the evidence and present it to me, until I have to agree with my own verdict of guilty.

However, God is also there in my one-man trial, and He is there as my defense lawyer, He is telling me the devil has it wrong, He will provide explanations, show me the good things and positive things, He tells me I am His, He tells me He has forgiven me, that the devil hasn't got enough evidence to convince so the trial needs to be thrown out.

Be blessed today as we remember scriptures such as **Lamentations 3:58 Lord, you are my lawyer! Plead my case! For you have redeemed my life and 1 John 2:1 and if any man sin, we have an advocate with the Father, Jesus Christ the Righteous.**

Winner man

One game that I am totally useless at is tug of war, I have no strength or grip so I would be of no asset to my team. Tug of war according to Wikipedia is a sport that directly puts two teams against each other in a test of strength: teams pull on opposite ends of a rope, with the goal being to bring the rope a certain distance in one direction against the force of the opposing team's pull.

It got me thinking, sometimes it feels like I am in a tug of war against myself, part of me is pulling away from God and church and the other part of me is trying to pull myself closer to God and church. Then is a part of me that feels like I'm in a tug of war with the devil, he is trying to pull me to the side of misery, pain, hurt, rejection, loneliness etc. and I am on the other end trying to pull myself into joy, happiness, love, self-acceptance, peace etc.

Sometimes I lose the game when I am playing by myself, but if I allow God to be on my team I can only ever win, the devil may pull me towards him and I'm one pull away from being on his side but God in his infinite strength shows up and pulls me back. There is no match against God's power and might.

I remember a couple of days ago I was organising some games and I said to a couple of people jokingly, only join my team if you can win, I don't do defeat lol, and then when my team was losing, I went and joined the winning side.

In life I need to choose God on my side, He will never fail, never lose. He can only win!!

It reminded me of a song by Ron Kenoly and it goes **'it is such fun to see, such fun to see Satan lose, Jesus is the winner man, the winner man, the winner man, the winner man all the time. I am on the winning side, the winning side all the time.'**

Be blessed today as you chose God to be on your side

Flying high

I hate flying with a passion, it's the turbulence that scares me the most, I think the plane is going to crash, Turbulence can be light, moderate or severe, but I've seen on films and TV programmes where the turbulence is frightening, as much as you or I may think the plane is going to crash, planes are designed to withstand the turbulence. It may rock the plane, may make it uncomfortable but it rides it out. Most planes will experience turbulence. The most common type of turbulence is clear air turbulence (CAT) You cannot see CAT. However, in severe turbulence the worst thing a pilot could do is try to fight it.

It got me thinking, sometimes in life we may experience some turbulence, for some it may be light, for some moderate and for some severe, our turbulence could be sickness, financial, mental, spiritual, relationship issues, work issues for example. Some of the time if our 'turbulence' is light to moderate we may be able to deal with it ourselves and ride it until things become calm again. But, if our 'turbulence' is severe, instead of trying to fight it and rock you from left to right, back and forth, instead sit back, and let the lord fight it for you. Turbulence on a flight does not last forever, it may seem like it does when you are experiencing it, but it must end, your 'turbulence' has to and must end.

In **2 Chronicles 20 it speaks of the Battle belongs to the Lord,** God cannot lose, the battle is already won.

Be blessed today as we trust God in our turbulent times

I know who I am

I remember watching a film a couple years ago called identity thief and as the title suggest, the thief stole another person's identity to commit fraudulent acts. Sometimes the identity theft can be for just a short period i.e., someone needed a new car so they stole someone's details, or, it could be a longer length of time, perhaps they may be wanted by the police or perhaps they want to start all over again where no one knows them.

It got me thinking, sometimes I feel like an identity thief, I am trying to be someone I am, I am watching others and trying to be them, stealing someone else's gifting, dress the way they do, talk the way they do, laugh the way they do, do what they do until I no longer know the real me.

I'm learning that its ok to be me and to not let the devil rob me of identity. God has said in His word that I am fearfully and wonderfully made, so if I believe His word to be true, why then do I want/need to be someone else as I'm already wonderfully made, can't' get better than that!

It reminds me of a song by Israel Houghton that goes **I know who I am, I know who I am I know who I am, I am Yours, I am Yours**

Be blessed today

Level up

I was playing candy crush the other day and was on a particular hard level, the level required me to collect a certain number of items before my opponent. I proceeded to start to play, and the game suggested a move for me to take, bearing in mind that the object is for me to win first, I took the suggestion and moved, but in taking that move it set up my opponent to make a better move than me! I got vexed because the game knew that move was not in my best interest. If I had ignored the computers suggestion, I may not have lost that level. Then there are times when although the move wasn't the best move in the beginning, it eventually led me to win the level.

It got me thinking, sometimes in life it can feel like I need to make a move and the enemy is dictating or suggesting what move I should take, sometimes like in the game I accept his suggestion, but his moves or motives for me good, they are not in my best interest, the moves he suggests are to make me lose. However, when God tells me to move it is for my good, I can but only win, His moves are for me to prosper, to grow etc. I may not see it at the time and wondering God why are you telling me to move here, but we walk by faith and not by sight and according to **Proverbs 3:5-6 we are to trust in the lord with all our heart and lean not on our own understanding.**

Be blessed today

Create in me a clean heart

The thing with the human body is that sometimes we are born with congenital problems or may develop them over the years, my sister was born with a hole in heart and had to attend hospital on many occasions, fortunately it wasn't that severe that it required her to have a heart transplant.

According to the internet a heart transplant is a procedure in which a surgeon removes a diseased heart and replaces it with a donor heart

Having a diseased heart can affect the way we live, our quality of life, can dictate what we can eat, what we can and can't do, we may also look unwell, and our life expectancy may be shortened etc.

It got me thinking before we became Christians, we could say that we had a diseased heart in a sense of us having a sinful nature, the things we done and said, our lifestyle and quality of life.

When we come to Christ and accept Him as our Lord and Saviour He becomes our heart donor, the heart doesn't need to be matched by blood type and our body won't reject it.

When someone has a heart transplant they can more or less live a full life, but unless they believe they have received a new heart they won't be able to enjoy the benefits of the new heart, they have to take the surgeons word that a new heart was given to them. The same way applies to us as believers, we have to believe that we have received a new heart and live a life according to that belief. We look healthier, our lifestyle changes our life expectancy becomes eternal.

Be blessed today

Do you love me?

As a child I remember playing a game with
friends to determine if someone loved us or not,
I don't know the correct name for the game, but
I call it he loves me, he loves me not. According
to the Wikipedia the game is a game
of French origin in which one person seeks to
determine whether the object of their affection
returns that affection. A person playing the
game alternately speaks the phrases "He (or
she) loves me," and "He loves me not," while
picking one petal off a flower (usually an oxeye
daisy) for each phrase. The phrase they speak
on picking off the last petal supposedly
represents the truth between the object of their
affection loving them or not. You hoped the last
petal fell on he loves me and if it did a big smile
went on your face.
It got me thinking, as a child we may have taken
that game literally and based our future
relationship on the pull of a petal. Sometimes as
a Christian, I find myself still playing that game
with God, I question does He love me or not,

this is usually based on how I feel about myself, if I have done something wrong or feeling lonely etc. and I'm like God do you love me?

However, loving us is not a game with God, He clearly loves us and there is no variation, no petal picking, no hoping and wishing, He loves us and **John 3:16 tells me that God so LOVED the world that He gave His only Begotten Son that whosoever believeth in Him shall not perish but have everlasting life.**

He cannot unlove us, He won't unlove us, God is love.

Be blessed today as you take comfort in knowing God loves you

Right to reside

As part of my job, I must determine if a person from overseas is eligible to claim and receive housing/council tax benefit. There are also times when I notice that a partner or family member has come over to the UK to reside with the family member already in the UK (A family member who joins you in the UK based on your right to stay in the UK is called a 'dependant', and you are known as the 'sponsor')

That partner/family member was allowed into the country because a family member is already there as a British citizen, so in effect they reap the benefit of this.

It got me thinking, as Christians even if our partner/family member is a Christian, it does not guarantee you access to heaven, you need to get there on your own merit. We can't rely on the good works or faith of someone else. It is an individual relationship we have with God; we are accountable for our own actions.

I'm reminded of the scripture in **Philippians 2:12 Therefore, my dear friends, as you have always obeyed--not only in my presence, but now much more in my absence--continue to work out your salvation with fear and trembling.**

Be blessed today

% content

I remember a while ago a Morrison's had some sausages that were being reduced, I thought I would give them a try. I cooked them and my son commented on how they tasted different, I replied that's because they are not cheap sausages. You can taste the difference between low pork content and high pork content sausages.

When I'm looking to buy sausages for example, I always check the 'pork' content, if its below 90% I tend not to buy it. If the sausages have 40% pork content, then I'm dubious what the other 60% of the sausage is made up off. Some name brand manufactures supply sausages with a low pork content but charge a lot for them. This surprised me as I would have expected the name brand to be off better quality.

It got me thinking, sometimes we can have preachers/pastors/bishops etc. who when delivering the word, their actual content is 30%

truth, you can 'taste' it as it doesn't sit right with you, it could even apply to well-known preachers- you think because they are well-known then what they are speaking is 100% truth but when you check the 'packaging' it's only 15%.

We need to be aware of what we are eating both physically and spiritually. Cheap food tastes cheap!

Proverbs 30:5 says every word of God *is* pure: he *is* a shield unto them that put their trust in him and John 17:17"Sanctify them in the truth; Your word is truth.

Let there be light

I was reading 2 Corinthians 6:14 yesterday and it mentioned what communion has light with darkness? And it got me thinking, light and darkness cannot work in conjunction with one another, one dispels the other, one counteracts the other, they are opposites not designed to work together, they work independently of each other, they each have a function.

Darkness makes everything black, it's hard to see, can make you feel gloomy, we often say have a dark cloud hanging over us, why not say light cloud? Darkness makes things hard to see or find, but it can also be of aid when you want to sleep, you need the darkness.

Light however brightens things up, we may feel less burdensome, we may say I feel as light as a feather as opposed to feeling dark as a feather. Light enables us to see things, find things, do more things.

For the last couple of days darkness has been my light, it has made the future hard to see, made it hard to find strength, hard to pray or read the bible. I just wanted the darkness to consume me permanently.

But just like the minute you flick on a switch, light a match, shine a torch, light a candle, darkness immediately goes, it must go, it's been counteracted by another source, even the tiniest light can make a difference.

I need Jesus to be my light and salvation, I need Him to be a lamp unto my feet and a light unto my pathway. I need the light of the world, the same God commanded let there be light, I need to command in my circumstance let there be light! Easier said than done at the moment

Keep me in your prayer's saints.

He knows my name

Anytime I speak to Bishop Lorenzo Jackson whether it be by phone or face to face he always greets me by saying "hello daughter", he knows my name, but he chooses to call me daughter, not sister Michelle as most church folk refer to me, but daughter, a father refers to their child as daughter, and that is how he makes me feel, he has owned me as such and it fills me with love anytime he says it.

It got me thinking, that's how God refers to me also, He calls me His daughter, when I speak with God it's like He is saying yes, my daughter, I'm here, I hear you, I love you, I want the best for you, I can help you etc., He has owned me as His, I belong to Him. God knows my name, but He calls me daughter.

My son never refers to me by my name, he calls me mom because that's what I am to him, I am not Michelle, I am his mom, his mother, his parent. It signifies the relationship we have and identifies my role.

I need to look upon God as my heavenly father and seek out a fatherly relationship with Him. He is patiently waiting for me to do that. I'm reminded of the scripture found in **2 Corinthians 6:18 that says "And I will be a father to you, And you shall be sons and daughters to Me," Says the Lord Almighty.**

Be blessed today

Opposites

Most things have an opposite, light/dark, hot/cold/ fat/thin, tall/small, wet/dry, in/out, good/bad, and so forth and it got me thinking, over the years I have felt pretty worthless, and I looked at what the word worthless means and it said 'having no real value or use. of a person) having no good qualities; deserving contempt, without worth; of no use, importance, or value; good-for-nothing' and to be honest that kind of summed me up. I was of no use nor importance to anyone; I offered no value and definitely had no good qualities. Things of no worth generally get thrown away. I felt I had been thrown away with the rubbish, but God looks at me as something valuable, the opposite of worthless is valuable and to be valuable means a thing that is of great worth, having qualities worthy of respect, admiration, or esteem.

God is saying to me I am valuable, I am of great worth, so much so that He sent His son to die for me. He sees my qualities, they may not all be good, but He is telling me and showing me, I have something good inside of me, He has not thrown me away, He sees my worth. An item that is valuable is taken care of, you don't want to damage it in case it becomes worthless, or God is taking care and protecting me. Some people even insure valuable items in the event the item gets lost/stolen etc. God has covered me; He is insuring me. HE WILL NOT LET MY WORTH BE DEVALUED...

Be blessed today, it's a battle but one day I will see and embrace my worth.

Stop!

I remember when learning to drive my instructor was teaching me about emergency stops, i.e., how to do one and in what circumstances it may require one. We would drive along, and he would say I will tap the dashboard and I want you to do an emergency stop. I didn't know when he was going to do it and my heart would beat fast in anticipation, then, bam, he hits the dashboard and I had to press my feet down on the clutch and brake pedals at the same time and the car came to a halt.

It got me thinking, emergency stops are useful to try and prevent an accident from occurring, you don't know when you will need to use it, but you know the process if the occasion ever arose. Sometimes as a Christian I need to adopt an emergency stop process, maybe I'm about to backbite or gossip, maybe I'm about to say something hurtful or do something to hurt myself or another person, maybe I'm on the

verge of leaving church or whatever the case
may be. God then bangs down on my dashboard
(could be my conscious, my mouth, my feet etc.)
and I come to an emergency stop. I've
prevented what could have been a catastrophe.

As a driver I never know what the roads will be
like or what other drivers will do, and likewise, I
never know what each day brings, and I need to
be always ready to do an emergency stop if
necessary.

Be blessed today

Who's the daddy?

I used to love watching Maury Povich back in the day especially when he was doing DNA tests and he would say "the DNA results show that xyz is NOT the father of abc. You would then get a mixed response from the 2 adults; one may weep with sadness and the other does cartwheels because they are happy the child is not theirs or the mom is glad the man is not the father. Sometimes on the show a woman would have 3 or 4 different men doing DNA test for the one child?

It got me thinking, we kind of have two DNA scenarios, one scenario is the DNA of sin. We were born in a sin and shapen in iniquity, as human beings we have a natural propensity to sin, this denotes our Adamic DNA, so we carry that in us, if we remain with the DNA of sin then according to John 8:44 You belong to your father, the devil, and you want to carry out your father's desires.

The second scenario we have is the DNA of God, whereby we have been born again, we have adopted His ways, in **Romans 8:14-17 it says For all who are being led by the Spirit of God, these are sons of God. For you have not received a spirit of slavery leading to fear again, but you have received a spirit of adoption as sons by which we cry out, "Abba! Father!" The Spirit Himself testifies with our spirit that we are children of God, and in 2 Corinthians 6:18 "And I will be a father to you, and you shall be sons and daughters to Me," Says the Lord Almighty**

I don't want my DNA test results to say I never knew you, depart from Me.

I want the results to be shouted out loud and clear for the whole world to see GOD IS MY FATHER

Repairable

 I saw a status this morning and it got me thinking; remember the nursery rhyme humpty dumpty and that after he fell no one could put him back together again?

 There are many of us who are broken, who come to God broken, who walk around living a broken life, most days I feel broken, I feel like I've been smashed into a thousand pieces and none of the pieces can be superglued together again. To be fixed you first need to be broken in the first place, that could be mentally, physically, emotionally, or spiritually. I long for the day when I will be whole. I've been broken for more years than I care to think about. Sometimes we go to the wrong people to get fixed or turn to the wrong things thinking they will fix us. In the nursery rhyme it said that all the kings' horses and all the kings' men couldn't put humpty back together again. It doesn't say how many horses and kings' men, but I would imagine it was in the thousands. What is hindering us from being fixed?

But we have a king that can put us back together again, in Jeremiah 17:14 it says God, pick up the pieces. Put me back together again. You are my praise!

I had an item that had a piece come away and I used some superglue to try and fix it, but the glue wasn't strong enough to fix it, I had to get the right strength glue! God wants to put us back together again, I know He is desperate to fix me, but to be honest, I'm fighting against Him. I want to be fixed but I don't want to acknowledge the broken pieces in order to be fixed

Be blessed today as we think of the song that says the potter wants to put you back together again, oh, the potter wants to put you back together again

Break it down

To get the contents from a coconut you have to break it open, to get your money out of a ceramic money box you have to break it open, to make a fried egg you need to crack open the egg shell, sometimes doctors break a person's bone in order to reset it or to make it grow a certain way, if we want habits to change then we have to break them. In order for a thief to steal your goods/car they have to break in. to get the nut out of a walnut shell you have to break it.

Sunday's message has still got me thinking today, to be broken is not necessarily a bad thing, as to be broken can produce something inside that we could not access/use unless it was broken.
There is no good filling up a money jar and then just looking at it, imagining all the things you could buy with the money, or wondering how much you saved, or telling people you have a full money jar at home but not going to use it...

pg. 226

what was the point of saving. The money jar, as pretty and as delicate as it may be designed to be broken, as that is the only way we can access what we have put in. the money jar when brought was just a vessel, not worth anything, once we started putting money in it, it became something of worth/value. You may not know how much but you know it has some worth purely by its contents. We have some much worth in us, so much value but we don't realise. Sometimes God has to break us to reveal our hidden treasure, I can't make a fried egg sandwich without first breaking the shell, I can imagine what the sandwich would taste like and how to cook it, but until I break/crack open the egg then it is off no use to me.

God needs to break us to show us what He has input in us, we may not know our worth or value, we may keep investing internally but not putting it to use, breaking an egg or coconut or money box can be messy, may have sharp edges, may leak liquid, but it's a process we need to go through to get what is inside. A thief will give it their all in order to break into a car/house, as they know the value of what they will come away with is worth the effort.

Let us trust God today as He breaks us to restore us to reveal to us that He has placed inside of us

Overflow

A cars petrol tank has the capacity to hold a certain amount of petrol/diesel, once that capacity has been reached, whatever extra petrol/diesel you try and put in the car will just leak out, the same as with a bottle, once it has been filled to its capacity any extra liquid will just spill out. A filled bath will leak out over the sides once full. I could give more examples, but you get my drift. We don't want there to be any overflow. Once we have filled up our car or bath, we use it until it needs refilling again. We are not going to fill a bath with water and then just sit and watch it, we filled it for a purpose, the same with the car, we filled it because we are going to use it. Imagine a bath or sink overflowing, the tap has broken, and you can't stop it and you run around trying to find buckets to contain the overflow of water.

It got me thinking, when we are asking God to fill us with His spirit, we need to then use it.

As mentioned above we don't want there to be any overflow, but, to me, there are some exceptions, the chorus 'many are the blessings that you give unto me, blessing overflowing like a mighty sea' and 'overflow, let your Spirit overflow'. To me this is saying that I don't want to restrict what God is pouring into me, I want it, I need it to overflow. I want my cup to runneth over just like in **Psalm 23:5. It states that a cup runs over when it cannot hold all that is being poured into it. Just think of all that waste running over.**

I want Gods love to overflow in me and in my life Psalm 23: shows how gracious and generous our God is, He doesn't provide just enough to fill the cup to the rim, He doesn't limit it to half a cup full, no, the CUP OVERFLOWS (not a physical cup). To first be filled, we need to empty ourselves of what is not of God. We won't need to be looking for extra buckets to contain the overflow

I read on the net that we can have overflowing joy, peace.

Be blessed today as you empty yourself in
readiness for the overflow

A change is coming

A caterpillar is a butterfly who has not realised it yet, this realisation only comes through the process of change, until it goes through the change process it will always remain a caterpillar. A caterpillar was always designed to become something else; it was never to remain a caterpillar.

It got me thinking, before we became Christians, we were caterpillars, however, once we accepted Christ, we are no longer caterpillars but butterflies in the making. (We are in the process of transformation)
God never designed for us to remain as caterpillars-a caterpillar is slow, moves at a slow pace, does not really do much, can easily be trod on, cannot really see high up, they make look ugly and when we were living in sin, that sin made us look ugly, caterpillars are usually eaten by other animals, and as such Satan is a roaring lion seeking who he can devour as found in 1 peter 5:8

On the other hand, butterflies on the other hand have a better advantage point, they can fly, reach higher heights, have more movement, it looks beautiful. The same applies to us as butterflies in the making, once that sin is removed from us, we now look beautiful, we can soar high (like wings on an eagle), we are no longer living under people's feet waiting to be trampled on.

We are not fully formed butterflies yet as in 2 Corinthians 3:18 we are being transformed into the same image from glory to glory, we are to be transformed into the image of God.

Be blessed today as we let God take us through the metamorphic process.

Royalty

I was watching the royal wedding on Saturday, and it was beautiful to watch, they both looked elegant and you could see the love being displayed. I bet Meghan must have been thinking, never in my wildest dreams would I imagine ending up marrying a prince and being a part of the Royal family. As I sat watching I thought to myself, fat chance of me ever marrying into the Royal family based on my ethnicity social standing.

But then I got thinking, I am part of the Royal family, my Father is the King of Kings, I am a chosen race, a royal priesthood

Revelation 17:14 states "and the Lamb will overcome them, because He is Lord of lords and King of kings, and those who are with Him are the called and chosen and faithful and Deuteronomy 10:7 says for the Lord your God is the God of gods and the Lord of lords.

Therefore, I am Royalty, my Father sits upon the throne. There is song by Donald Lawrence that goes "Don't you know that you are royal greatness, chosen to reign to lead with holy wholeness, you are an heir, you are royalty, destined to protect your land, you are an heir, embrace your legacy.

We may not have the expensive white dress, or the millions in the bank, no, we have something much greater that money cannot buy. We have a mansion waiting for us, we have a Father who will supply our needs according to His riches in glory.

Be blessed today as you realise your worth. YOU ARE ROYALTY!

I do

Back on the theme of the royal wedding, I looked at Prince Harry when he met Meghan at the altar and all through the service you could just see him staring at her in admiration and pure love. He was just on love.

It got me thinking, God loves us more than the above scenario, He loves so much more that He gave His ONLY begotten Son to die for us. That's how much we are loved by God. We may not have our bride or groom to look at us with the look of love like Prince Harry and Meghan, we may not have the wedding photographs to reflect the loving ceremony, what we do have however, is a God who was willing to sacrifice His son for us, we have a Son who was willing to be sacrificed, bruised, battered, ridiculed and humiliated, we have a God who gives us His grace and mercy, we have a God who forgives us of our sins, we have a God who provides for us. We have a God whose love will never ever end. In 1 John 4:8 it declares God is love, God loves us. Sometimes people who get married who were once so in love, end up getting divorced because for various reasons the love has now gone. We have an assurance that God will never stop loving us despite our faults, despite us not living right, despite us neglecting Him. His love is unconditional.

You may think, well, God doesn't love me, let me tell you He does, He declared it in **John 3:16 For God so loved the world that he gave his one and only Son, that whoever believes in him shall not perish but have eternal life.** Therefore, that scripture means God's love is inclusive of everyone.

Be blessed today as we reflect, remember, and hold on to the truth that God loves us.

Bless me Lord

I remember when it was my son's birthday,
and we would play pass the parcel game
and imagine when it stops on your go you
are frantically tearing at the layers. You get to
the layer where the prize is and you're about to
rip the paper to get the prize out and the music
starts again and you have to pass the parcel
on, and then the next person when the music
stops gets the prize. You get upset because that
prize should have been yours. You were robbed,
just 5 more seconds and it could have been
yours.

Or you're playing the game and the music
stopped on you and again you're frantically
tearing at the layers and then the music starts
again but you're not ready to pass the parcel as
you can see the prize and you want it, but the
person next to you snatches it out of your
hand and passes it along.

It Got me thinking there's a song that goes bless me lord bless me, what He blesses cannot be cursed, no man can take the blessing from you. When God has something for you, then no one can snatch it out of your hand, I suppose it's a bit like when you open your phone with your fingerprint, no matter who has the phone, only you can access it. Only you can open the phone to access what's inside

I saw a quote on the internet, and it said when God pronounces a blessing, it's a done deal. Nobody can revoke it or change it! The only thing that will stop the blessing of God on your life is disobedience to God's Word. But if you're walking in obedience, then the blessing of God will be on your life!

Be blessed today

Never alone

I remember years ago I was in town with my son and he ran off into a shop, one minute he was walking beside me and the next he'd gone, the panic and fear that I felt was indescribable. I couldn't find him, I called his name, I searched the shop and even asked staff if they had seen him.

Or there has been times when I'm at a shopping mall trying to meet up with someone, I can't find them, so I ring and get their location but still can't find them, and panic sets in.

Lately, I have been feeling lost, feeling God has left me, like the example with my son, it felt one minute God was walking beside me and then suddenly He had gone, I called out to God, I searched for Him, but I couldn't find Him, I felt alone, abandoned.

It got me thinking, God never leaves us, we may leave Him, but He never forsakes us. When my son ran off, it was him who left my side, it was him who made the move, I hadn't gone nowhere, I hadn't left him. He left me.

I remember on Friday feeling terribly alone and people were saying you are never alone, God is always with you. I didn't want to hear it because I couldn't feel it. I couldn't feel Him. But, if we are to walk by faith and not by sight then I have to believe that when God says 'Lo I am with you always' then that is what He means, not I am with you sometimes, or only during 9-5, but always, when I'm hurting, when I'm scared, when I'm happy.

Just like the T in merlot or the K in know, it may be silent, but it doesn't get removed from the spelling. God sometimes may be silent in mine and your lives, but it doesn't mean He has removed Himself from us.

Deuteronomy 31:8, The LORD himself goes before you and will be with you; He will never leave you nor forsake you. "Do not be afraid; do not be discouraged.

It's getting hot in here

In this current heatwave, the sun has knocked me out, I remember walking into town on my lunch breaks and because of the heat I felt faint, I felt weary, I was dragging myself along, I just never had any energy, or, when I was at the gym (when I used to try and keep fit) I would go on the treadmill for say half an hour, but after 10 mins of running I grew tired, I hadn't the strength to carry on running, so my running became walking and my walking became a stroll until eventually out of tiredness I gave up.

It got me thinking, in life we are bound to feel weary, feel faint, feel weak. Even athletes must grow weary during a marathon or 1000m run, but, even if they do they persevere, sometimes in a race you see the athletes sprint off so fast that after the first lap they are tired, whereas you may get other athletes who start off slow, but as they see the finish line approaching, they gather their strength and take first place.

There's been times in my spiritual walk that I have grown tired, don't have the strength, feel like I've walked or come as far as I can go, but the song reminds me that I can't give up now, I've come to far from where I started from.

Just like the athlete above who has run 9990m out of 1000m and thinks, I can't give up now, I ran too far, I've walked to far, he pushes himself, he knows he needs to carry on, he may stop temporarily and refresh himself, may stop temporarily to gather more strength, but he stops in order to keep going. Sometimes we have to stop fighting, stop using our own strength, stop and be renewed, stop and let God be our strength, stop and let Him fight our battles, stop and wait on the lord, stop and hope in the lord, THEN, we will not grow weary, nor faint, but SOAR.

But those who hope in the LORD will renew their strength. They will soar on wings like eagles; they will run and not grow weary; they will walk and not be faint. Isaiah 40:13

Phantom pain

I've never had a leg or arm amputated, but I have read stories from those who have, and they mention something about phantom pain. according to the internet Phantom limb pain (PLP) refers to ongoing painful sensations that seem to be coming from the part of the limb that is no longer there. The limb is gone, but the pain is real.

It got me thinking, since my mom died, I have experienced pain, it feels as if a part of me has been amputated, the limb is my mother, she has gone but the pain is real. That part of me has gone, it can't be re-grown, can't be reattached.

After amputation some people may be offered/given what is known as a prosthesis- which is an artificial device that replaces a missing body part. Prosthetics are intended to restore the normal functions of the missing body part.

Years ago, the artificial limb was quite basic, you could tell it was artificial and I suppose didn't really offer much use to the person, but it replaced a part of the body that was missing, nowadays, technology has developed and some of the limbs are mid blowing. It takes the person a while to get used to the limb and how to function it and accept it as part of their body.

I have had people in my life over the years who have become like a mother to me, who have replaced my missing limb- my mother, just like the above scenario it has taken me a while to accept that these 'mothers' love me and want to be a part of my life and accept me.

Today is a difficult day, a very lonely day, a very reflective day, a day when I wish my' limb was never amputated'.

God says He will never give us more than we can bear and today I need His strength.

Fruits

At our ladies' night at church there were a range of different fruits such as lemons, strawberries, pears, melon etc on the table, we were a bit intrigued as to why they were there and also hunger set in for me lol.

We were then asked individually what fruit we would pick that best describes us, I chose the melon because although it has a hard exterior/shell, once you cut it open it has a soft centre, I have a hard shell on the outside to protect me from being bruised/damaged/hurt. People may see this in a negative way, but, once you open me up (not literally) I have a soft inside, I am loving, caring etc.

If you dropped the melon onto the floor, unlike a strawberry, it won't smash or be squished. Its exterior protects it, you don't know what is inside until you open it. People won't get to know me by just making judgement on my shell.

Sometimes we do and I do it myself, when I'm buying fruit sometimes you look at the outside, try and smell if it is sweet and then make a judgment call based on that, sometimes it works, other times it doesn't.

At bible study a couple weeks ago we were looking at the declaration of faith and touched on the fruit of the spirit. Bishop John Jackson asked us how many fruits of the spirit were there and answers ranged from 7 to 9 to 11. But Bishop replied and said there is only one. I looked at him in disbelief, no, there are 9 fruits!!!!

But when I re-read **Galatians 5:22-23 it says but the fruit of the Spirit is......** doesn't say fruits!

Bishop then went on to give an example of a Satsuma, it is one fruit but once peeled there are different segments to the one fruit. I never viewed it like that, was very eye opening and made me realise that the Satsuma is a whole fruit, we don't go out and buy segments of the fruit, likewise, the fruit of the spirit is one and we should be aiming to have all those different segments in our lives daily.

Galatians 5:22-23 But the fruit of the Spirit is love, joy, peace, forbearance, kindness, goodness, faithfulness, gentleness, and self-control. Against such things there is no law

He's in control

When watching certain films that involve a boat, dinghy, or canoe for example, 9 times out of 10 once they reach their destination, and usually it's some beach in the middle of nowhere, they climb out of the boat and in the blink of an eye the boat drifts out to sea. Either they were too slow in tying it up or they didn't tie it securely and now they are trapped.

It got me thinking, if I am not tied securely to Christ, then I am bound to drift away, If I am not tied securely in my prayer life, bible study, church attendance and relationship with Christ, I will drift away. I may think I am tied securely but if after 2 weeks I've not prayed or studied or communed with God, little by little the devil will come in and start to gently drift me away.

I'm not going to lie, these past few weeks have been difficult, and I've felt myself drift, but don't feel I have the strength to pull myself back to safe ground, to re-tie myself. I want to be drifted away.

Have you ever seen a person walking their dog and they have this lead that lets the dog walk quite a way in front but the owner can still draw the dog back by adjusting the lead? The dog probably thinks he has his freedom, but he is still under control of the lead. Or a toddler who has a harness on them, they may be able to walk independently by not holding their parents/care givers hand, but they are still under control. As much as I feel I am drifting away God has me, I don't believe He will let me drift off permanently or too far, I am under His control.

There's a song by Kirk Franklin that goes 'He's still in control, He's sovereign and He knows, just how it feels to be afraid, have folk you love walk away. Be still and know He's still in control.

And the well know song we have an anchor that keeps our soul, steadfast and sure while the billows roll

I'm having to trust God will keep me anchored. I
need Him too desperately

Come unto me

I saw this video on Facebook and it was about a
baby who was born with no arms or legs and
was left in an orphanage, eventually a family
adopted her, however, whilst watching the
video it made me realise just how helpless the
child was, they could do nothing for themselves,
they could barely lift their head up, they would
be reliant on help for the rest of their life.

It got me thinking, God never leaves us helpless,
He always sends someone to assist, you may not
realise they have come to assist you, it may not
be a physical act, it may be a word, a financial
gift, a hug, a dinner invite. God can see and
know that the situation we are in may leave us
feeling helpless, that we can barely lift up our
head. These last couple weeks I have felt
helpless, and I have been wondering God why
have you left me feeling like this, why have you
left me to pick up my head when it is so
burdened and heavy that I can't.

Scriptures such as **Psalm 121:1 I will lift up mine eyes to the hills from whence comes my help, my help comes from the lord, and psalm 42:11 why are you cast down o my soul and Hebrews 4:6 let us therefore come boldly to the throne of grace, that we may obtain mercy and find grace to help in the time of need.**

The last scripture is to me an action scripture, it is saying I need to COME and not just come but BOLDLY come to the throne of grace. If I come but come timidly or weak then fear can continue to creep in, but if I come boldly, it shows that I am coming in a confident and courageous way.

Be blessed today as you boldly come to the throne of grace in your time of need.

Something out of nothing

When a mosaic piece is finished it looks beautiful, however, in order to get to the finished product, the artist may spend hours assembling small pieces of glass or stone together. So, imagine you break a coloured vase, its shattered into tiny pieces and to you it is now useless, it's broken, no longer has any use and you don't have the desire or patience to fix it. But, to an artist, that broken vase is a masterpiece waiting to be created, to them it needed to be broken for them to use it, an unbroken vase is of no use to them. They specialise in broken things. The artist will gather the pieces and have already visualised the result.

Sometimes in life I feel like that broken vase, I'm shattered, my heart is shattered, I've been broken beyond repair, or sometimes feel that I am too much of a pain for others to want to spend time with me to help 'fix' me. But an artist came along, picked up my broken pieces and is painstakingly assembling the pieces into a work of art. The artist doesn't see me as broken, doesn't see me as shattered and useless, He sees me as a warrior, an overcomer, a survivor. He sees me as His child and wants to spend the time restoring me. He has the patience; He has the glue that will hold me together.

In **Psalms 51:16 we are reminded that a broken and contrite spirit, thou wilt not despise, O God." And in Psalm 34:18 The Lord is near to the broken-hearted and saves those who are crushed in spirit.**

Be blessed today as we trust God to create something beautiful out of us.

Plaster it up

When my son was younger and he cut himself, no matter how big or small a cut, he wanted a plaster on it, sometimes some cuts need a plaster on it, but other cuts they need to breathe and get the fresh air on them, putting a plaster on it may delay the healing process. Putting a plaster/bandage on also hides the cut so it's not visible to others; the only sign that you are hurt is the bandage/plaster.

This got me thinking, sometimes in life we have been cut through hurt, being used and/or abused, being damaged etc., and if I focus on myself in particular I have had many a time I wanted to bandage/put a plaster on my hurts and so forth, I want to cover them up so I can't see them, I didn't want to see them, they wasn't visible for anyone to see them but my facial expressions or my low mood was the only sign to indicate I was cut, but, in my opinion there are some cuts that we need to expose, we need to leave uncovered so that the healing process can begin. God can't heal us if we cover things up from Him, yes, He already knows but He wants us to bring it to Him. I'm on a journey where I have to uncover my cuts to let the healing virtue flow.

Be blessed today as we are reminded by the words of Beverley Crawford's song **'let the healing virtue flow, touch every heart, bless every soul, according to faith let it be so, the wounded are made whole, from infirmities and woes, when the virtue of the Lord begins to flow'**

Split ends

One Friday at work in October, we had some
stalls in support of black history month, there
was one stall that was selling a family made hair
oil. The woman selling the oil had beautiful long
hair and said it's all attributed to that hair oil.
What better advertising do you need, someone
with super long hair looking healthy, why
wouldn't you buy it. It worked for her so it must
work for me, right? Nothing to do with the fact
of her origin or that everybody's hair is different
and grows at different times and lengths.
This got me thinking, over the years there have
been loads of adverts or recommendations from
people to say this hair product is the best, this
shampoo will do this, or this treatment will do
that. I've gone through a few different products
hoping my hair will have the desired effect it
offers. But I've realised that not everything the
product claims to do it actually does. I have
been growing my hair for a while and it's got
to a decent length, but I also had very bad split
ends, I knew that they needed to be cut off as

they were stunting new growth, but in cutting those off I would lose the length, but keeping the length was doing more damage. Sometimes in life we need to cut off our split ends, they could be friends, habits, swear words, relationships, behaviour. Sometimes we may feel and look like we are growing spiritually, but, due to our split ends we aren't actually growing, it's a false representation. Cutting off the split ends helps your hair from further splitting and the health of the hair is maintained which as a result makes it grow longer and stronger.
Likewise cutting off our spiritual split ends will in the long run help us grow stronger and maintain a healthy relationship with God.

Be Blessed today as you cut your split ends.

Plans

Sunday evening, I was at national convention and just behind me there was some commotion and all I heard someone say is "she's died in her seat", I turned round to see what was happening and an elderly lady was unresponsive, her daughter was grabbing her and shouting "mommy, mommy, no mommy". It was heart-breaking. At a first glance it appeared that the lady had passed away during convention that thankfully it was low blood sugar levels which caused her to pass out.
On Monday there was a lot of traffic, at least an hour and half were added on to people's normal journey home, some people were angry at this, others just sat back and waited. Later in the evening I found out that a cyclist had been crushed by a lorry, hence the reason for queues as some roads were closed whilst paramedics could attend.
On Tuesday morning I read that the cyclist had tragically passed away, she was only 32, my heart was sad, and it got me thinking. This lady

was riding I assume home, she may have said goodbye to her work colleagues, rang family to say I will be home in 40 mins, may have even been thinking what she will cook for dinner later that night, I don't think she thought or imagined that she would not make it home.

We are not promised tomorrow, we are not even promised this evening, I make plans daily, what I'm going to watch when I get home, what am I going to eat, what needs washing etc., I am expecting to reach my destination, but in proverbs 27:1 it says do not boast about tomorrow, for you do not know what a day may bring and in James 4:14 it says yet you do not know what tomorrow will bring. What is your life? For you are a mist that appears for a little time and then vanishes. We all have been given an expiry date, we don't know when, I remember there's times when people would say to me "I'll call you next week or I'll see you tomorrow God willing of if God spares my life" and I'm like erm ok, but I understand the context in which they say it. ▨

We never know when our expiry date has come, unlike milk or food we now when its shelf life has finished.

Be blessed today and I will write another blog tomorrow if God spares my life

Unfriend

Growing up one of the worst things you could say to me was "I'm not your friend no more". To hear those words meant your life had ended. I would write notes to the person or try and do sneaky calls begging them to be my friend again. I was distraught. Needless to say, we eventually became friends again, and, over the course of the years, friendships ended and restarted. There was also a time when you had to have a best friend, that one friend who knew you inside out, who you could tell anything to, who would be the first person you call if your upset, angry etc., you placed them higher than your other friends.

As I got older and more so in recent years, certain friendships have ended, new friendships created, I remember when my son was younger, and I would tell him off and he would reply "I'm not your friend". To Him that was a powerful statement, he had fallen out with me, and he expected me to be hurt. I simply replied, that's ok cus I'm still your mother.

Sometimes I say to Jesus I'm not your friend, I have fallen out with Him, and He's like no problem because I'm still your Father. Sometimes I get a bit upset because I feel I don't have a best friend, but if I think about it, I do, I just don't remember or fail to use it. Jesus should be my best friend, He knows me inside out, He should be the first person I go to when I'm upset, when I'm angry, I can confide in Him, tell Him anything. The song that goes 'closer than a brother, my Jesus is to me, He's my dearest friend, He's everything I need' should remind me that this is a friendship unlike others in the pass will never end. The only way it will end is if I end it, Jesus is a friend for all eternity. Again, the song that goes 'And I'm overwhelmed that you would call me friend' resonates within me today.

Be blessed knowing you are a friend of God, and, if you're not, God is extending His friendship to you today

Bribery

There's been a few occasions in my house where my son may ask me for something i.e., money or new trainers, and before I give him an answer, I ask him if he has done what needs doing, i.e., have you washed up the stuff from 2 weeks ago, have you put this away.
(Dependant on his answer, is dependent on what reply I give him) His reply is always the same, I'm not being bribed. My son wants something from me, but he hasn't done anything to deserve it.
It got me thinking, sometimes, well a lot of the times God gives us things that we don't deserve, we haven't done what we have supposed to, but God is not like man, so He doesn't always respond/provide/answer according to our actions.
Other times we may want God to do something for us and we may say God if you give me xyz then I will do abc, or we may want God to do something in our lives and God may be saying, well, have you done what you have meant to

have done. It doesn't mean that God is bribing us, He may have given us a task or instruction prior, and we haven't acted upon it, but we are asking for more.

Be blessed today

Happy birthday

Sometimes I've been given gifts and I'm like thanks, but I don't need it, or I don't know what to do with it, so the gift just sits there unused. Out of all the gifts that I have been given over the years, love is the hardest one for me to accept, I don't know what to do with, I know I need it but when it comes, I'm like ok then. Yesterday when I should have been celebrating my birthday, up until 7pm I had spent the day practically in tears, I couldn't explain why, I didn't even know myself, I just felt so down. I knew I should be grateful God spared my life for another year, I was blessed, I lacked for nothing so the question why art thou cast down o my soul? People would probably say why you are miserable on your birthday but for me sometimes my emotions don't care what day of the week or what occasion it is. It was a bittersweet day for me.

Questions kept going through my mind as to why would you and why do you love me, do you not see how unlovable I am?

It was so intense, I couldn't deal with it, but, as I sat down to my birthday meal and I looked at the people that were there, my friends and family, I became more overwhelmed, it was such a lovely evening spending time with those that love me beyond my faults, beyond my failures. I remember texting someone and they said they would be able to come to Birmingham especially if it is to see me. The greatest birthday gift, Christmas gift, any gift anyone can give me is the gift of love, that is priceless, has no expiry date, will have use in countless situations. I NEED IT!! I just need to first accept the gift, then unwrap it, and then use it.
I thank you all for your kind words and birthday wishes......its fab being 31 but it's more fab being loved.

Be blessed

Mental Health 2

So, it was mental health awareness day last week and I contemplated whether I should write this post, but I decided to write it anyway as it's something I find is not spoken about and more so as a Christian I feel the guilt twice as much. So, in the mind of Michelle Bailey part 2 imagine you have just walked past somebody, and they start laughing to the person next to them, well, obviously in my mind they are laughing at me, why are they laughing? It must be because I'm ugly that's why or because my hair is a mess, my clothes don't look right. Do I blame them, no? because what my mind is telling me is truth, or, if someone at work sends an email and immediately someone else burst out laughing, then that email is about me, about what they think of me, how they don't like me, how I'm annoying, ugly, miserable, always eating. Have I seen what was on the email? No, but the email was about me because my mind is telling me it is so it's the truth.

Or I'm walking in town and I see another female walking towards me, no matter how nice I thought I looked 2 mins ago, I now look at myself with contempt, I hate me, why does she look so feminine, why is she so pretty, why is so slim, why am I so fat, this is why nobody wants to marry me, I'm just so ugly, is it true?, yes because my mind has told me so it's the truth. I then spend the rest of my time in town with tears in my eyes, avoiding eye contact with anyone and thinking what is the point of living. To cope with these situations sometimes I go home, open my beside drawer, pull out the tiny silver razor and cut myself, with eat cut I remind myself how worthless I am, how much I am hated by people and so forth. Does it help, yes, is it right, no, do I feel guilty after, yes.
I know some people won't understand and will say your body is a temple so it's not yours to mark and you're pretty and so forth, but the problem when you suffer with mental health, well for me anyway is that I want the pain to go and I need to feel an external pain for the internal pain. I write this and open up myself so

I can say to someone else, you are not alone. I know I feel alone very much most of the time

Be made whole

So, I'm re-reading the book of John and am
currently on chapter 5 and in particular the
crippled man by the pool of Bethesda. I have
read this passage many times but this time I
used a bible commentary and it opened it up in
a whole new way.
And it got me thinking, I had thought the man
had lived by the pool his entire life and that the
water was troubled by the angel daily, I was
wrong, the angel only came at certain times
which I am led to believe was when feasts were
on (maybe a yearly feast).
There have been a few occasions when I have
been at church and when the altar call has been
given someone will come out of there seat, take
my hand, and lead me to the altar, and, just like
the crippled man, he had to have his friends
bring him daily to the pool so he can get his
healing. He could not get there by himself, he
wanted to go, but he couldn't, there's times I
want to go the altar, but I feel crippled by my
sins.

When the waters were eventually troubled in the pool it was I imagine a fight to get in there first, the crippled man knew he wanted to get there, but by the time he may have had help to get to the water his chance had gone, this spoke to me and said of the man's determination, 38 years I imagine he was waiting for his healing, hoping that this time it would be him.

The commentary also said that Jesus asked the man if he wanted to be made whole, sometimes we think we want to be healed but deep down maybe we don't, this man was a beggar and it was his source of income, if he became whole maybe his income would go, sometimes we may want deliverance from an addiction but then we think what I will do without it.

What really spoke to me though was this, Jesus was at the pool, His presence was there, their eyes were fixed on the water, expecting it to be troubled; they were so taken up with their own chosen way that the true way was neglected." (Spurgeon)

So I have decided to read the book of John again and I used a commentary this time and wow did it open it up.

I was looking at the scripture of the crippled man at the pool of Bethesda and it got me thinking on the following things:

- He waited in hope for 38 years for his healing
- He was determined
- He was dependent on others for his healing
- He never gave up
- He had faith
- He was obedient when Jesus said take up your bed
- He witnessed
- He knew Jesus

Sometimes I feel like the crippled man in the sense that I have been waiting years for my healing, but I haven't always been determined and may faith hasn't always been at the level it should be, I felt that other people could bring my healing so I was dependent on them for prayer, that they, like the angel that would trouble the water so the sick could step in and be healed, they would trouble the water for me.

I gave up, I wasn't obedient, sometimes at the altar when pastor has prayed for us, he sometimes says go and believe your healing or whatever you have asked God for, I went away doubting. Jesus asked the crippled man if he wanted to be made whole, sometimes I feel Jesus is saying to me, Michelle, do you really want to be made whole? If you do, only I can make you whole. When Jesus was at the pool of Bethesda, the sick people's eyes were fixed on the water, expecting it to be troubled; they were so taken up with their own chosen way that the true way was neglected." (Spurgeon). I too, fail to sometimes see that Jesus is standing right there; ready to heal me but I look to my own ways and miss the opportunity.

There has been a few occasions when I have been at church and when the altar call has been given someone will come out of there seat, take my hand and lead me to the altar, and, just like the crippled man, he had to have his friends bring him daily to the pool so he can get his healing. He could not get there by himself, he wanted to go, but he couldn't, there are times I want to go the altar, but I feel crippled by my sins.

The angel only came to trouble the water on certain times, possibly yearly at the feast/Passover, so the sick only had limited opportunities to be healed. Jesus doesn't come at certain times, He is here. God never leaves us or forsakes us, He is patiently and eagerly waiting to heal us, He is asking us today- "Do you want to be made whole?"

I leave you with the lines from a song by Karen Clark Sheard:

'He is here, God is here, to break the yoke and lift the heavy burden, He is here, God is here, to heal the hopeless hearts and bless the broken, o come lay down the burdens you have carried, for in the sanctuary God is here'

Keep clear

 Yesterday I was driving home and approached a set of traffic lights, the section of the road had a yellow box junction. I waited patiently for the lights to go green and then got vex, although it was my cue to move, I couldn't because some van decided to block the road by being stationary on the yellow box. I was stuck.

The rule for this junction is that you MUST NOT enter the box until your exit road or lane is clear, however, you may enter the box and wait when you want to turn right and are only stopped from doing so by oncoming traffic or other vehicles waiting to turn right (the Highway Code).

Blocking the yellow box prevents others from moving forward, stops the flow, creates traffic, blocks the way ahead

This got me thinking, sometimes people can be like the van mentioned above, they may come into our lives and park, themselves in the yellow box in our life, and we may not see or know the block is there, but they do. They block us from moving forward. Some people for whatever reason may not want to see us prosper; they may be jealous and try to prevent us.

Upgrade

After months of deliberation, I finally brought myself a new phone, it's much faster than my old one and can do slightly more things, however, after my initial excitement; I had to refer to the manual. The reason being is that I didn't know what the phone's full potential was. I knew the basics it could do but that was all, I even watched some YouTube videos as there were people who knew more about my phone than I did.

This got me thinking, sometimes I don't see my full potential, I know some of the basic stuff, but I don't know full what I am capable of, so, I need to refer to the owner's manual-God. He made me, created me, formed me, knows all about me and what I can do, He knows the hidden stuff. Then there are some people who like those on YouTube can also see the potential in me, they can show me and say Michelle I see this in you, or I know you are capable of doing this.

I remember laughing with a friend once because they had a phone and just use it to text and make calls and I said you shouldn't have a phone as you are not using it to its fullest, you are not utilising it. Sometimes it feels like God is saying to me, Michelle, what I have given you, you have not utilised it, if you did it would open a whole new world, or it may make your life easier or help you get through this season/trial. Who knows the iPhone better than the creator Steve Jobs? Who knows Microsoft better than its creator Bill Gate? Who knows us better than our creator God?

When I brought my phone, I spent a lot of time researching at what it can do, likewise I need to invest time in myself to see what I can do.

Jeremiah 1:5 says before I formed you in the womb I knew you, Psalm 139:1 O Lord, you have searched me and known me, Ephesians 2:10 for we are His workmanship, created in Christ Jesus for good works, which God prepared beforehand, that we should walk in them.

Mommy's touch

Do you remember when we were kids and we had cut ourselves, even if it was the tiniest of scratches or a gaping wound, we would go running to our mom (usually our mom) or guardian and ask them to kiss it to make it better, you had tears streaming down your face, were inconsolable, you were dying! But all it took was one kiss on the wound and we were made well. The tears suddenly stopped, and we carried on with whatever we were doing. It wouldn't be the same if it as your cousin or aunty for example kissed the wound. Only your mother or guardian could make everything ok. When I look through the bible and see all the miracles and healings Jesus done, all it took was one touch or one word from Him and they were made whole. They may have tried other sources for their healing such as those who dealt in magic or soothsayers but only Jesus could make them whole.⏃

There have been times when I've asked others to pray for me, and whilst that is not a bad thing, if I want to be healed, I have to reach out and touch God for myself, only He can do it. Only He can make me whole. The woman with the issue of blood, she touched Jesus once and was made whole, somebody else couldn't have touched His garment for her, when Jesus opened the eyes of the blind, He laid His hand on their eyes, only He could do it. One touch or one word is all it took.

When you touch fire you feel its heat, when you touch ice you feel its coldness, when you touch something coarse you feel its roughness, when you touch silk, you feel its smoothness. When you touch Jesus, you feel His power!

There's a song by Fred Hammond that says **"one touch is all it takes to be made whole, reach out and touch the Lord he's passing by, don't miss this precious moment touch the Lord and be made whole"**

There is also a chorus **that says reach out and touch the Lord as he passes by.** To touch something or someone involves an action, you

have to reach out to whatever you want to touch.
Be blessed today as you touch the Lord

Free Money

I have been watching a programme recently called money for nothing, and basically the presenter visits a rubbish tip where people are throwing away unwanted items. The items may be old, used, worn out, has no purpose for the owner no more. The presenter then goes around looking at the items and picks out a few that they see has potential and takes them away. Those items are then sent to the experts to upcycle/recycle the items and transform it into something else, something of use. Sometimes after it has been transformed, they take the item back to the person who threw it away and they are surprised at what it now looks like. It is completely new.

It got me thinking, there is many times I feel used, worn out, fit for nothing, has no purpose and ready to throw the towel in on life, but God steps in, sees the potential in me and upcycles me, He transforms me and when He has finished

transforming me, I am better than before. I know have a purpose and can be used.
This also applies to our mind, my mind sometimes is filled with information that is old, of no use to me and God transforms my mind and in **Philippians 2:5 it says "let this mind be in you, which was also in Christ Jesus"**
2 Corinthians 5:17 Therefore if anyone is in Christ, he is a new creature; the old things passed away; behold, new things have come.

Be blessed today as you remember God has a use for you and can transform you

Mental health 3

The problem with my mental health is that
sometimes I find it extremely hard to cope with
my emotions, imagine you have a tap that can't
turn off properly, so it drips constantly all day
and all night, you try to drown out the sound or
ignore it but you know it's there. Or imagine you
can hear a cricket in the grass, you can't see it to
move it, but it's there making a constant noise.
Not going to lie this past week has been
challenging, my mind hasn't switched off, I've
felt threatened, I've felt scared, my mind was
working more than overtime, it was plotting to
kill me, that would have been the best outcome.
I couldn't even say to my mind PEACE BE STILL! I
couldn't talk to no-one, and no one actually
truly understood. How can you explain to
someone else when you can barely explain it
to yourself? An animal or a baby for example
cannot tell you verbally when they are in pain or
where the pain is, they make suggestions i.e. cry
or whimper, they may refuse food, and
they may not use that particular limb. They

know they are in pain; they want you to know they are in pain, but the communication is blocking the transmission. I couldn't communicate to anyone the sheer deep distress I was in. suicide seemed the only option.
Last night I felt I was drowning, I was being drowned emotionally, I couldn't find or see the lifeguard, I was like Jesus where are you? Throw me the life jacket. My emotions imprisoned me; I'd be given a life sentence without parole. I was dying. I cried so much I grazed my eye. Mental health comes in all shapes and sizes and guises, I can look you dead in the face and say I'm ok, I'll even smile when deep down I'm plotting how I can hurt myself. Mental health is nothing to be ashamed off and you shouldn't feel guilty for being affected.
I share this not to expose myself, but to let another person who maybe feeling the same that they are not alone, I feel alone because mental health is real, it is real for Christians, and it is real for me. Peeps I truly need your prayers, my fight has gone, my energy has gone. I don't want my hope to be gone

Deleted

Every now and then I like to clear out my phone by removing messages, photos, and videos. Sometimes when I go to delete it, I get a message asking if I want to permanently delete it as once it's gone, I can't get it back. Or there have been occasions at work where I have completed a document in error, and to get that document back I have to seek permission from my team manager to get that document reinstated. If I needed to get a text message back on my phone after I deleted it, I would most likely have to go to my phone provider and request it. I don't have the authority to do it myself.

It got me thinking, when we ask God to forgive us from our sins, we are in effect asking Him to permanently delete them from us, and if God permanently deletes them, only He has the power to reinstate them, and, since He doesn't reinstate them, why are we trying to override that authority. It's not ours! He no longer remembers them as stated in **Hebrews 8:12 'For I will forgive their wickedness and will remember their sins no more'.**

Sometimes my son has a habit of saying "mom, remember when you……" ▯and I'm like oh yeah, I remember, when we try to get our sins back from God it's like saying God remember when I stole or lied etc., God's like erm no because I have forgiven you and remember it no more. Wow, if God who is above all things can remember our sins no more, how much more should we do the same? I speak to myself because I'm forever reminding myself daily of sins I have done.

In Psalm 103:12 it says He has removed our sins as far as the East is from the West.

Be blessed today

I'm not perfect but that's OK is a compilation of Michelle Bailey's blogs.

To follow Michelle's blogs connect with her on Facebook and search for the page **I'm not perfect but that's OK**

Printed in Great Britain
by Amazon

81600003R00169